*TWAYNE'S WORLD AUTHORS SERIES*
*A Survey of the World's Literature*

# BRAZIL

Luis Davila, Indiana University

**EDITOR**

*João Guimarães Rosa*

TWAS 506

João Guimarães Rosa

# JOÃO GUIMARÃES ROSA

## By JON S. VINCENT

*The University of Kansas*

TWAYNE PUBLISHERS

A DIVISION OF G.K. HALL & CO., BOSTON

Copyright © 1978 by G. K. Hall & Co.

Published in 1978 by Twayne Publishers,
A Division of G. K. Hall & Co.
All Rights Reserved

Printed on permanent/durable acid-free paper and bound
in the United States of America

*First Printing*

**Library of Congress Cataloging in Publication Data**

Vincent, Jon S
Joao Guimaraes Rosa.

(Twayne's world authors series; TWAS 506: Brazil)
Bibliography: p. 173 - 78
Includes index.
1.   Rosa, Joao Guimaraes, 1908 - 1967 — Criticism and
interpretation.
PQ9697.R76Z93    869'.3    78-19151
ISBN 0-8057-6347-3

For Sean and Tanya

# Contents

# About the Author

Jon S. Vincent received both the B.A. and the Ph.D. at the University of New Mexico. Currently Associate Professor of Spanish and Portuguese and Associate Chairman of the Department of Spanish and Portuguese at the University of Kansas, he has also had visiting appointments at the University of New Mexico and the University of Costa Rica. Professor Vincent first went to Brazil in 1959, when he studied for a year as an undergraduate on a program sponsored by New York University. As a graduate student, he spent a year in Portugal as a Fulbright Fellow and returned to Brazil for a year of research as a Title VI Fulbright-Hays Fellow. Since his appointment at the University of Kansas in 1967, he has directed K.U. summer language institutes in Mexico and Brazil and the K.U. academic year program in Costa Rica. He is a member of the Advisory Board of the K.U. Center of Latin American Studies and Chairman of the K.U. Committee on Luso-Brazilian Studies.

His principal research interest is contemporary Brazilian prose fiction, but he has maintained an interest in Spanish American literature. He serves as an Assistant Editor of the *Latin American Theatre Review*, and is currently working on a study of Brazilian vanguardist fiction of the twenties and thirties.

Professor Vincent has published articles and reviews in *Hispania, Modern Language Journal, Luso-Brazilian Review, Latin American Research Review, Journal of Interamerican Studies and World Affairs,* and *The Brazilian Novel* (Indiana University Publications). This is his first book.

# Preface

João Guimarães Rosa had published five volumes of fiction when he died in 1967. Two more were released posthumously. These seven works should constitute a major landmark in world fiction of this century, but because of the somewhat limited accessibility of the books most of the attention they have received in this country has been from specialists. Access to them is limited, first, by the fact that they were written in Portuguese, which unfortunately remains a language of less than great literary prestige; secondly, by the fact that the Portuguese in which they are written is so dense and convoluted that the prose presents serious problems of comprehension even to many Brazilians. But even if they cannot or will not read his books, almost all literate Brazilians know Guimarães Rosa's name, and most of those who have gone to the trouble to do the reading are almost worshipful.

Several of the books are available in translation in the major European languages (English, French, German, Italian, and Spanish), but in no language are there more than three. Those translated have sold respectably but not spectacularly; internationally, the most vocal enthusiasm for Guimarães Rosa seems to have come from other writers and from the translators themselves. A reading of the three works now in English would provide a reasonable basis for an appreciation of the writer's talents, but it would not really be enough to admit a full appreciation of what the Brazilians and the translators are so excited about, because it would not give a full sense of reading the same three in the original. That has always been a limitation of translations, but I think it fair to say that in this case the translators have had to make more than the usual compromises, and that the results of those compromises are not poor translations but books which accomplish things different from the originals. It is no doubt excessive to preface a critical study with the admonition that readers of the study take the time to learn another language before proceeding further, but I know of few writers more worthy of that effort than Guimarães Rosa. Realizing that not many will want to go to the trouble of learning Portuguese, I have provided translations of titles and citations where no English version is available, and in one case I have provided a retranslation.

It is probably apparent that my enthusiasm for this body of work is high, and I confess that I have very likely not maintained a consistent ironic distance from the subject, since it is one which has given me many hours of illumination and frustration. But I have tried to resist, perhaps not always successfully, the impulse to gush, and I have also tried to resist the impulse to disguise my personal preferences as disinterested judgments. Insofar as possible, in fact, I have attempted not to make any such value judgments at all. With a writer like Guimarães Rosa, it is probably fair to say that a scale of relative valuation from volume to volume is even more useless than such things ordinarily are, because every one of his books merits a second and third and fourth reading, and every one changes in the process.

I have also attempted not to frame the study in a specific critical method, since it seems to me unproductive not to allow a certain eclectic latitude in discussions of writers of great technical range. I have, however, directed most of my attention to what happens to readers, or what I think might happen to readers, in the process of reading the books. That is, I have dealt with literature as experience rather than as social commentary or philosophy or something else. Somewhat arbitrarily, I have attempted to frame each work in terms of a feature of that volume which in my own readings seems to have been of particular importance in understanding and appreciating the book. The selection is arbitrary in the sense that the features chosen are in a degree applicable to the whole of Guimarães Rosa's works, but I have attempted to identify in each chapter a salient feature of the volume under consideration which might be of use in viewing that book on a trajectory of the complete work.

Throughout the study, I have attempted to give some indication of each book's critical reception in Brazil. On occasion, I also make reference to Spanish American writers, principally because Guimarães Rosa has been identified as the Brazilian most closely associated with what is called the "boom" in Latin American fiction. Again to provide a point of reference, I have mentioned a handful of books in English. I have made less reference to other Brazilian writers, on the assumption that many readers will not be familiar with them, and also because I think Guimarães Rosa deserves to be considered a sort of solitary national genius, belonging to no school and having no real disciples.

Guimarães Rosa was a doctor of medicine, a diplomat, a polyglot (he spoke six languages and read fourteen others), an amateur naturalist. He was also a humanist. Some say he was a mystic. Whether or not any further information about his life would prove illuminating is debatable, though some of his critics have made interesting contributions based on biographical data. The fact that he was myopic as a child and later wrote about myopic children and that he practiced medicine and wrote stories told to doctors may be evidence that his works were a reflection of his life, but the way these stories operate in the reader's consciousness makes it seem to me that our knowledge of his visual acuity and professional training is largely irrelevant. It might help to remember that he was born and raised in Minas Gerais, the Brazilian state thought to produce the most introspective thinkers, that he spent some years in the interior as a practicing physician, that he was a respected member of Brazil's diplomatic corps. A number of other facts are worth mentioning just because they are interesting, particularly those regarding his obsessive love of languages: living in the relative isolation of the Brazilian interior, he started reading French at the age of six; later, as a young man, he no doubt surprised and pleased a displaced White Russian he happened to meet by insisting on hearing for the first time the correct pronunciation of a language he had already taught himself to read; he improved his Russian further still when a Cossack Chorus showed up to give a show in the town of Barbacena. But clearly the most interesting thing about his life was that he wrote extraordinary books, and they are the subject of this study.

I would like to express my appreciation to the University of Kansas for providing me with summer research grants which allowed me to begin this book and for a sabbatical leave which allowed me to finish it. My thanks also to various of my colleagues who took the time to read portions of the manuscript and offer suggestions for improvement. They are not responsible for any lapses, because I have not always followed their suggestions. Special thanks to John S. Brushwood and George W. Woodyard, who patiently digested virtually the entire original manuscript and offered their counsel.

My thanks also to the University of Wisconsin Press for permission to use "Corpo de Baile," *Luso-Brazilian Review*, 14, no. 1 (Summer, 1977), (© 1977 by the Regents of the University of Wisconsin), pp. 97–117, which was the basis for chapter 2 of this study.

JON S. VINCENT

*The University of Kansas*

# Chronology

1908    June 27: João, son of Florduardo Pinto Rosa and Francisca Guimarães Rosa, born in Cordisburgo, Minas Gerais, Brazil.

1918    Enrolled in the Colégio Arnaldo in Belo Horizonte, Minas Gerais.

1925    Began the study of medicine at the Medical School of Minas Gerais in Belo Horizonte.

1929    Became a public servant, working for the Statistical Service of the state of Minas Gerais. His first literary publication, "O Mistério de Highmore Hall" ("The Mystery of Highmore Hall") appeared in the magazine *O Cruzeiro* on December 7. Three more of his short stories were published in later numbers of the same magazine.

1930    June 27: Married Lygia Cabral Pena. December 21: Graduated from medical school.

1931    Set up private medical practice in Itaguara, Minas Gerais.

1932    Volunteered to serve as a doctor with the *Força Pública* ("national guard"). Participated in the Constitutionalist Revolution in Belo Horizonte and later competed for, and earned, the position of staff physician for the *Força Pública*.

1933    Became medical officer for the 9th Infantry Battalion in Barbacena.

1934    July 11: Passed Foreign Service Examination and entered the Ministry of Foreign Affairs.

1937    June 29: His volume of poetry, *Magma*, won the poetry award of the Brazilian Academy of Letters. It has never been published.

1938    His one-thousand-page manuscript entitled "Contos" ("Short Stories"), which was written in seven months, won second place in the Humberto de Campos contest. Some judges and at least one publisher were interested in publishing the work, but the author, who entered the contest under the pseudonym "Viator," could not be located. May 5: Named Vice-Consul in Hamburg, Germany. Here he met Aracy Moebius de Carvalho, who became his second wife.

1942   January 28–May 23: Interned in Baden-Baden. Returned to Rio. June 22: Named secretary of the Brazilian Embassy in Bogotá.

1944   Returned to Rio.

1945   Named Head of the Brazilian State Department's Documentation Service. In five months of intensive work, his "Contos" were transformed into *Sagarana.*

1946   *Sagarana,* half the size of "Contos," published by Editora Universal. June: Named Secretary of the Brazilian Delegation to the Paris Peace Conference.

1948   Secretary General of the Brazilian delegation to the Ninth Pan-American Conference in Bogotá. Named First Secretary of the Brazilian Embassy in Paris.

1949   Named Counselor of the Brazilian Embassy in Paris.

1951   Returned to Rio as Cabinet Chief of the Ministry of Foreign Affairs.

1952   Accompanied a cattle drive from Andrequicé to Araçaí, Mato Grosso, and published his "report" "Com o Vaqueiro Mariano" ("With Cowboy Mariano").

1953   Became Budget Chief of the State Department.

1956   January: *Corpo de Baile (Corps de Ballet).* May: *Grande Sertão: Veredas (The Devil to Pay in the Backlands).*

1957   Unsuccessful candidate for membership in the Brazilian Academy of Letters.

1958   Promoted to Minister First Class, with rank of Ambassador.

1961   Received award from the Brazilian Academy of Letters for collected works.

1962   Named Chief of Borders Division of the Brazilian State Department. August: *Primeiras Estórias (The Third Bank of the River and Other Stories).*

1963   Elected unanimously to membership in the Brazilian Academy of Letters.

1965   Brazilian Representative to conference on Cultural Relations in Genoa. Participated in the First Latin American Writers Conference in Mexico City as Vice President.

1967   July: *Tutaméia (Trifle).* November 16: Formally seated in the Brazilian Academy. November 19: Died.

1969   November: *Estas Estórias (These Stories).*

1970   November: *Ave, Palavra (Hail, Word).*

### CHAPTER 1

# Sagarana: *Transcendental Regionalism*

O NE of the hoariest and most cherished pedagogical devices employed in discussions of Brazilian prose fiction has been a categorization of every work into one of two broad types: rural fiction or urban fiction. The advantages of such a division are immediately apparent, since a number of legitimate and necessary distinctions can be assumed to proceed from a work's categorization as one type or the other. Not many books escaped this labeling operation, and even works which seemed to have elements of both forms, such as the novels of Graciliano Ramos, were fit into one of the categories by means of a distillation process intended to make the divisions more specific. The initial step in refining the definition consisted of yet another admirably simple assumption, one so frequently supported by the writers themselves that it became one of the maxims of Brazilian literary history. Reduced to its essence, the assumption was that there existed not only two sorts of fiction, usually distinguishable on the basis of theme alone, but two approaches to the writing of fiction as well—one a cerebral, introspective, and "universalist" treatment cultivated mostly by urban writers; the other largely descriptive, picturesque, social, and particularistic, written for the most part by writers from rural backgrounds. The surgery was also facilitated by a tacit assumption of cultural tradition: city writers were thought to have descended from the cultivators of the aestheticist and vaguely aristocratic isms (such as Symbolism and Surrealism) which contributed the cosmopolitan flavor to Brazilian Modernism; rural writers were thought to have a necessary affiliation with Romantic Indianism, Realism-Naturalism, and assorted species of social and political literature. The few exceptions, such as Mário de Andrade's *Macunaíma*, were easily dealt with, because the prime corollary to the dogma of separation evolved into a refinement of authorial treatment of theme and technique. Thus, although *Macunaíma*'s hero is born in a remote tropical forest and the book is shot through with Tupi myth and stereotyped characters, the cerebrations of the citified author are always apparent: structure fails to provide the necessary linearity, the social message is hidden or at least vastly complicated, there are alternations between the real and the surreal, and finally, the *simplicity* necessary for localistic fiction is lacking. The apparent regional character of the work is at last seen to be nothing but a veneer on a book intended for a small cosmopolitan readership, and *Macunaíma*, albeit with some difficulty, was pushed into the corner of the aestheticists.

Until recently, this scheme worked almost too well, and in some quarters still does, because the second and unspoken corollary is merely that the first category is written by and for real intellectuals, the latter by and for a larger and supposedly somewhat more raffish group. But the more precise elements of the definition, including the treatment of theme (the general versus the particular), style (real versus surreal, local versus universal), characterization (typical versus atypical), ethical base (social versus spiritual), and at last the question of mimetic literature versus genetic literature still operated and continued to be employed without much difficulty by critics of a wide variety of aesthetic inclinations.

In Brazil, the first work to do real violence to this scheme was a book of short stories composed in 1938 and published finally in 1946 under the title *Sagarana*.[1] Every page of the book is laden with elements of the Brazilian *sertão* (a word which, roughly speaking, refers to the "backlands" in Brazil. See note 1 of chapter 3 for a fuller discussion of the term). There are animal characters, cowboys, bandits, magic spells, and a whole series of linguistic and technical features drawn from the traditions of Brazilian regionalism. But there was just no legitimate way to give the category its customary good fit. There were some annoyingly sophisticated features, similar in some ways to the features of *Macunaíma* yet lacking that book's combination of intellectual pretentiousness and playfulness, which made the categories seem suddenly unworkable. Although the stories in *Sagarana* are drenched in local color, it would be not only unfair but downright wrongheaded to describe them as "regionalist" and no more.

With *Sagarana*, Guimarães Rosa accomplished what Mário de Andrade only made an eccentric foray into in the twenties. The product is similar to one variety of work produced in the "boom" in Spanish America. Mario Vargas Llosa, Alejo Carpentier, Gabriel García Márquez, and a number of others have written and continue to write a kind of fiction rife with deceptive simplicities and unexpected complexities, but they share with Guimarães Rosa a vision, a style, and a technique which have in large measure demolished the urban-rural dichotomy as a critical starting point. The treatment of theme, style, characterization, the ethical base, the simplicity and complexity have become fused, and it now seems hardly worth the effort to set about making the distinctions any longer.

Parallels with other Latin American writers will undoubtedly occur to readers familiar with these works, but a real analog is unlikely. Not even in Brazil has another writer managed such a perfect fusion of the localistic and cosmopolitan, and most Spanish American writers are comparable only by fragments. In Guimarães Rosa's prose the form and the process are of sufficient novelty to make a qualifier such as "neoregionalism," overly general, since the term has been used for so many varieties of recycled provincialism. A coinage more accurately descriptive of this kind of fiction might be "transcendental regionalism."[2]

Guimarães Rosa's aversion to the predictable and his passion for the past are apparent from the first glance at *Sagarana*. The title itself is a neologism, an agglutination of the Germanic root which gave the name to the Norse saga, and a Tupi suffix meaning "rough, crude."[3] The book opens with a story entitled "O Burrinho Pedrês" (translated as "The Little Dust-Brown Donkey"). Below the title appears a curious epigraph from a "solemn rural song" and, in the original Brazilian edition, a drawing of a donkey loaded with an immense burden. Below the donkey is a large infinity symbol. The donkey and the symbol are enclosed in a heavy circle. The careful reader is thus warned that the story he is about to read is likely to involve a cosmology ampler than the one ordinarily associated with humble beasts. The text is related by an apparently omniscient third-person narrator, whose diction combines the picturesque elements of folk speech with the suggestivity and playful inventiveness of a poet-linguist. Riddled with alliteration, neologisms, syntactic reversals, internal rhyme, and ellipses, the narration proceeds to recount the tale of Seven of Diamonds, a feeble old donkey which has been conscripted as a mount for one of the cowboys on a cattle drive. The last choice as a means of transportation, not solely because of his age but also because of his breed, Seven of Diamonds goes on the journey only because of the shortage of horses and gets a rider only because the rancher so orders.

With the exposition barely made, the narrative begins to wander off into other matters, some with no apparent relation to the main story line. This tale can, in fact, be separated into two basic parts, one dealing specifically with the burro and the other consisting of side narratives. Less than a third of the story deals directly with the animal protagonist.

The plot line which follows the donkey is relatively simple, at least after a second or third reading in which the subplots can be pruned away. Seven of Diamonds serves as a reluctant but reliable mount for one of the cowboys on a cattle drive, and the herd successfully reaches its destination. But a swollen creek complicates the return trip, and the men decide to wait for the lagging donkey, whose well-known intelligence in such matters will settle the question of whether to cross or not. The climax of the story cannot be fully explained without reconsideration of the main subplot, because at this point the structures of the two apparently unrelated main narratives cross, and the irony of the denouement is lost without the complementary elements.

The human characters are involved in a conflict involving two cowboys who are rivals in a love interest, and it is feared that one of them, Badú, is likely to end up dead as a result. Badú, insensibly drunk, has the bad luck to reach the horses last, so he ends up with the least desirable mount—Seven of Diamonds.

The donkey and his unconscious passenger finally reach the creek, and after a moment's hesitation, Seven of Diamonds enters the water. The others follow. Eight men and their horses die in the flood. Saved is Badú, who crosses still mounted and asleep, and the foreman, who grabs the donkey's tail in desperation and is dragged ashore by the dauntless beast. The two other subplots in this story function, like the epigraph, rather like musical flourishes, a counterpoint and an elaboration of the ironies suggested in the tale itself.

Because of the very relaxed pace of the narration and because of these apparently unrelated asides, some critics have doubted that this is a short story at all. Fábio Freixeiro suggests that because of these factors and because of the "psychological richness" of the narrative, it is impossible to call it a short story. Since it also lacks novelistic structure, however, he finally applies the term *novela* to

"O Burrinho Pedrês," although it seems that Freixeiro is not using the term in the sense of "novelette" but rather with its vaguely pejorative connotations of popular and entertaining fiction.[4] Freixeiro goes on to classify the story as one of "space and character," an interesting conclusion in view of the concept of "transcendental regionalism," since exactly those elements would be the fused polarities of the two sources of this mode of fiction. Most of the stories in *Sagarana* fail to meet the standard criteria of the short story, in fact. The paring to essentials of structure, time, place, and characters which produces the brief illumination of a fragment of reality is absent here. But also lacking is the almost self-indulgent pace the structure of a novel can allow. A seemingly unrelated tale about a bull, for example, has some very specific functions in the outcome of the tale, and the proximity of this aside to the total structure is greater than at first appears. The telling of the tale and the reactions to it are major parts of characterization in the early part of the tale, when the bulk of the narrative is in dialogue. More important, the eventual climax of the aside, which occurs near the dramatic climax of the tale, is the source of a series of illustrative parallels in which the main story line is both illuminated and enhanced by the metaphors, aphorisms, and object lessons hidden in the digression. Functioning as framing devices, these fictions within the fiction serve both to expand the limits of reality and to make more plausible the central narrative. The heroic and magical nature of the asides also increases the final irony, in which the least significant of the creatures is the vehicle of salvation for two of the least likely, and perhaps least deserving, of the human characters.

The masters of the Brazilian short story have not been strangers to the nineteenth-century dictum that the *sine qua non* of good writing in the genre is economy of expression. Guimarães Rosa chose in this work to ignore that rule, but it would be pointless to attempt to edit his stories down, because even the distillate form would probably not quite fit the generic criteria. The book's next tale confirms the suspicion that the narrative tradition from which much of the work derives is more than a step from the nineteenth-century local colorists. More than any other tale in the book, "A Volta do Marido Pródigo" ("The Return of the Prodigal Husband") is a demonstration of the curious means employed by Guimarães Rosa to advance the art of the narrative. To go forward, the first step is backward, but not to the previous century. Here it is to a deeper tradition, one in fact at the very roots of narrative fiction—the oral folktale. The structure and many of the narrative conventions of this tale are those of the trickster tale, which has parallels in most cultures with a literature, written or not. In the United States a close pseudofolk parallel can be found in the Uncle Remus tales. In Brazil there are both folk and erudite cycles concerning Pedro Malasartes, whose nearest Spanish American parallel would probably be Pedro de Urdemalas. This tale's protagonist, like most tricksters a lazy but engaging scoundrel, is the mulatto Lalinho Saláthiel, sometimes employed on the road gang building the Belo Horizonte-São Paulo highway. Lalinho decides one day to work not at all rather than sporadically, and suddenly leaves his job and his beautiful wife and departs for Rio. After six months, he returns to find his wife living with a Spaniard and his chances for gainful employment slim, but a local politico recognizes his potential and takes him on as a ward heeler for the upcoming election. By deceit, trickery, and the appropriate use of threat and humility, Lalinho finally manages not only to guarantee the politician's reelection but also to get his wife back. As a bonus, he succeeds in having the Spaniard (who, as a foreigner, he informs his boss, cannot vote) evicted.

Freixeiro again settles for the term *novela* to describe this story, again used with its soap-operatic connotation. He sees little aesthetic importance in the tale, and concludes that part of the reason for its lack of impact is its developmental reliance on action.[5] The tale admittedly suffers more than any other in the volume from a certain cuteness, but as it is an updated folktale, the rather transparent linearity of the plot and outlandish accomplishments of its protagonist are consistent with the tradition. There are also fragmentary parallels with the picaresque tradition in this tale, especially those of the protagonist's origins, nonprofession, and eventual triumph over difficulty through use of his only notable talent, his wits. Though apparently limited in terms of cultured reader appeal, this story of a silver-tongued Brazilian rogue and his rival, the Spaniard, entertains without indulging in the esoterica of local fauna, custom, and lexicon. It is also noteworthy that, true to the tradition from which it springs, this tale is in large measure a tone piece, in which incongruities of occurrence and exposition are manipulated by the narrator for humorous effect. Thus, aside from such frames as the toad myth, which North Americans will recognize as Br'er Rabbit's briar patch motif, the tale's effect relies on the meandering pace of the storyteller and the incongruent hyperbole of style, as when the narrator indulges in a description of so simple an event as the receipt of a telegram by Lalinho's employer, Major Anacleto:

And the message had evolved from a Draconian-despotic-coercive style into a cabbalistic-statistical then into a Messianic-palimpsestic-periphrastic, and then into a homely-friendly-memory-jogging, and thus, from pot to plate, from funnel to bottle, the fine initial stock turned into a thick broth, very nourishing and efficacious; all this in parentheses, to show one of the reasons why politics is an easy air to breathe—but only for those accustomed to it, for the uninitiated stifle in it and give up.(90)

The next tale, "Sarapalha" ("The Straw-Spinners"), is more easily identified as a short story, largely because of the rigidity of structure and reductive treatment of theme, space, and character. The story deals directly with only two characters, and what little action there is takes place in a single day, though important segments of the tale are related as remembered episodes. The two protagonists, referred to throughout the tale as "Cousin Ribeiro" and "Cousin Argemiro," speak only in fragmentary dialogue in the first third of the story, and the reader's information is provided largely by a narrator privy to their knowledge of happenings. The exposition establishes the atmosphere and provides information about the major event in the life of the village, the arrival of a virulent malaria epidemic. Coincidental with the arrival of the epidemic is the major event in the lives of the protagonists, the departure of "Cousin Luísa," Ribeiro's wife. This past history is then juxtaposed to the present, and most of the rest of the tale consists of dialogue between Argemiro and Ribeiro or a reproduction of their thoughts. Both are in the terminal stages of fever, and their interdependence has grown to the point that their seizures are synchronized, so that one can care for the other during the daily crises. And every day, during Ribeiro's delirium, Argemiro tells him a story. It is always the same story, one which tells of a maiden lured into the canoe of a handsome swain who turns out to be the Devil.

But Argemiro fears that his own feverish ramblings will one day cause him to reveal his long-kept secret—that he too loved Luísa. Rather than letting the fever do the deed for him, Argemiro decides on this special day to confess. Ribeiro, his trust and honor sullied, orders Argemiro away, probably to die in the woods, while he remains to die where he is. At this point the only other active character in the story, the dog Jiló, suffers his own crisis. He can no longer remember which of the two is his true master, and he cannot decide whether to stay or go.

Freixeiro classifies this tale as a short story of emotional effects, with an overlay of atmosphere. Because of its structure, he categorizes it as a "short story-memoir."[6] But the major effects are not all emotional. Although the story is structurally quite simple, its most striking feature is probably that of the fused characters. In the initial part of the tale, the narrator takes advantage of the gender system of Portuguese nouns to elaborate an interesting personification of the several feminine synonyms for "malaria," and the characters then proceed to identify that personage with their own female interest, Luísa. Since she is at last the real cause of their deaths (as is malaria), the love theme is distorted both by their ambivalence toward her and toward the disease. Behind the love story is the code of honor, which might have been merely picturesque but turns out to be another element of both tension and ambiguity. Both men have been dishonored, since both loved Luísa, and either should have killed her and/or her lover. Argemiro has dishonored Ribeiro by loving Luísa but maintained honor by taking no action. The tale within the tale is a brief recapitulation of one of the temptation motifs common to folk literature, but to the characters it is an ironic source of strength while they wait for death. Since the dialogue is either fragmentary or semidelirious, the reader is at times pressed to remember who is talking to whom, and the dog's confusion at last confirms the merging of the two protagonists. The symbiotic relationship between them and the underlying concept of the honorable way out are thus both more interesting and more important than the emotional effects. Such effects are considerably reduced, in fact, by the inevitability of the outcome and by the attitudes of the fused character. Though not quite a story of ideas, "Sarapalha's" structural proximity to that of the parable likewise indicates the predominance of the moral question over other considerations.

"Duelo" ("Duel"), the next story in *Sagarana*, is undoubtedly one of the most entertaining of the narratives, though perhaps not the most artistic. Apparently a third-person omniscient narration, this story is an early example of Guimarães Rosa's talent for disguise.

The narrator is obviously not Guimarães Rosa himself, because the tone and content of the impersonal narration are those of the backwoods raconteur. Again, much of the tale is in dialogue, and that not in dialogue is interspersed with occasional flashes of folk wisdom and assurances to the reader that the story is a true one, which of course only makes the reader more doubtful. The tone is by turns jocular and serious, the pace leisurely. This is the first of several of Guimarães Rosa's works to be based on the quest motif. In this case, the quest is one of revenge for an affront to the local code of honor, a frequent theme in *Sagarana*. The protagonist of the story is Turíbio Todo, a saddlemaker with a foul dispostion and a small goiter. The story opens with his having a bad day: he loses his fishhooks while fishing, stubs his toe, and finds his wife in bed with a soldier. Vengeful but not stupid, Turíbio does nothing at the time, preferring a more leisured revenge with a clear and unretaliated shot at the offender, Cassiano Gomes. The next day his plan goes perfectly, except that when he does arrange for the clear shot he squarely hits and cleanly kills not his cuckolder but Cassiano's innocent brother. Now the stage is set for the duel, because Cassiano is bound by both hate and honor to kill Turíbio, unless of course Turíbio kills him first. The chase goes on for months, with exchanged mounts, accidental crossings of paths, near misses, and mistaken identities. The duel becomes the cause célèbre of the *sertão*, most of the locals rather favoring Cassiano because of Turíbio's cowardly gunfighting style. Counting on his antagonist's weak heart to take care of the killing for him, Turíbio executes a strategic withdrawal to São Paulo, returning only when he hears news that Cassiano is finally dead. Nearing his home, Turíbio is overtaken by a harmless-looking little rustic named Twenty-One, to whom Cassiano had served as protector during his final days. Twenty-One has assumed the burden of Cassiano's revenge, and when the two riders stop for water, Twenty-One produces a derringer and dispatches his enemy-by-proxy with two bullets.

Freixeiro accurately labels "Duelo" a plot or action story.[7] Like its regionalist predecessors, the tale maintains reader interest through the traditional sequences of rising action, climax, and denouement, and it also shares many of the picturesque tendencies of earlier fiction. The narrative is rich in folk wisdom, and events frequently impel either the narrator or a character to unleash some homely aphorism appropriate to the occasion. Much of the imagery is also drawn from rustic sources, although the source alone fails to reduce imagery to picturesqueness. The language of this story, in fact, is one of the most interesting aesthetic features, and one which prevents it from being merely another rewriting of the rural revenge tale. Another interesting feature is the author's manipulation of time, since, unlike the usual short story, the chronological span here is rather protracted, amounting to something like a year. In a sense the tragic potential of the tale is mitigated by the comic, because of tone and because the story is something of a comedy of errors. There are dozens of mistakes made by characters in the tale, but structurally the story turns on an axis of just a few. The first is Cassiano's mistake of taking Turíbio's wife at an inopportune time, the second, Turíbio's mistake in identifying his intended victim. Cassiano then errs in overestimating himself and in underestimating his adversary, and later repeatedly rides for days in the wrong direction in his misguided pursuit of Turíbio. In the second part of the tale Turíbio first commits the obvious error of not considering Cassiano's intent to arrange for a replacement, then the climactic error of returning unguardedly the moment he hears of Cassiano's death. The motive force behind all the action, including most of the mistakes, is the code of honor, in many senses reminiscent of the unwritten code which has been the theme of so many bad cowboy movies. But this story has a saving grace in its linguistic virtuosity, and another in the deft control of irony, which as usual has several facets. The ironic tone is the most obvious feature, but there is also the dramatic irony of the denouement, and finally a larger irony involving the theme. Turíbio is presented by the narrator in the beginning as a "bad" man, but his actions throughout the tale are those of a man acting properly if somewhat less than courageously in terms of the codified system of honorable behavior. Cassiano's only real sin is a rather minor one, consisting of no more than placing the horns on Turíbio's head. But he is honor bound to carry out all further actions. Both are largely sympathetic characters, so that the final irony of the tale is the elimination of all the characters of strong reader identification and the curious and unpredictable means by which the two deaths come about.

Mary Daniel has written that an important characteristic of *Sagarana* is the "underlying charm" of its stories.[8] "Minha Gente" ("Mine Own People"), the book's next tale, is a rather fragile story in which the author's ability to charm is tested, because there is relatively little of real substance in the story-memoir. Here the transformation of remembered detail suffices to be charming, but the tale lacks the intensity of later works, perhaps because it depends more on reminiscence itself than on the imprint left by the past. The narration is in the first person, and the narrator's rural background and city education, plus the diarylike tone, mark this as the most autobiographical of the stories in this book. The exposition contains the narrator's throughts on returning to his country home after years of absence, and is framed by a mobile chess game in which the narrator and the local chess fanatic indulge while riding toward the ranch. The narrator succeeds in placing his adversary, Santana, in a hopeless position, but here the game is interrupted, to be finished by correspondence, and the main story begins.

The principal sequences concern the narrator's developing amorous relationship with his cousin Maria Irma, although the political maneuverings of Uncle Nascimento are also prominent. There are also several other subplots, such as the curious story of one Bento, a fishing companion of the narrator's. As much lover as fisherman, Bento ends up dead at the bottom of the fishing hole one day as a result of his philandering. The narrator's love life, by contrast, is merely frustrating, and he finally goes off to visit neighbors to nurse the hurts caused by Maria Irma's constant rebuffs. During the visit, he receives two notes, one from his uncle, announcing a landslide political victory; another from Santana, who has finally figured out how to extricate himself from the chess game a winner. The chess move described by Santana gives him an idea for furthering his frustrated romantic conquest, and he gallops back to the ranch. He finds Maria Irma in the garden. With her is the gorgeous Armanda, with whom he immediately falls in love and later marries. Maria Irma marries her patient boyfriend Ramiro.

Freixeiro criticizes this tale for being poorly structured, and claims that it attempts to be a short story of emotional effect but that the effect is dissipated by the "grafts" of other plot lines.[9] Guimarães Rosa's considerable talent for successfully carrying out such grafting operations is apparent in other stories, and especially in his later works, but here it may be that the theme does not deserve such elaboration. The chess game itself is an appropriate frame for the tale, and is deftly handled, especially at the end. As a sort of metaphor for the love game, the chess game also provides the tale with some of its better comic moments, as when the narrator describes Santana's prodigious memory for anything to do with chess and his complete disregard for all other matters:

I had to laugh. Not at Santana's ability to remember the games by heart, nor at his capacity for ignoring the long lapses of time, thanks to which one day I will see him pull out of his pocket the case, this very same case, and propose to me the continuation of that game—subvariant K of the Belgian variant of the Sossegovitch-Sapatogoroff system of the Yugoslav semi-frontal counterattack of pawn to knight to queen—interrupted ten years before precisely at the nineteenth move. (147)

In addition, the apparently gratuituous tale of Bento Porfírio is a foreshadowing, although the narrator is obviously unaware of this. Bento's fondness for angling was his ruin in more ways than one. He passed up the first chance to meet the object of his affections when he thought a few days of fishing would be preferable to a blind date. Later, he met the girl and immediately fell in love with her. But by then she was already married, so he married on the rebound and subsequently enjoyed his true love extramaritally, ending up in the bottom of the pool as a result. This tale within the tale is a counterpoint to the main story line, and the naive and sentimental narrator fails to understand the true dimensions of love until the end. Maria Irma, it should be noted, understood this all along.

The admittedly diluted nature of the emotional effects and the insistence on concepts, games (chess, fishing, and love), and color, suggest, in fact, that perhaps the "grafts" are not as inappropriate as might be thought, since the story seen in this light is one of idea and of atmosphere. It also has something of the flavor of the collective character sketch. That these features place it very close to its regionalist predecessors is not to be denied.

The next story, "São Marcos" ("Woodland Witchery"), provides a foretaste of the linguistic jungle Guimarães Rosa would subsequently allow to flourish, an attempt to expand the language to a point where it would be adequate to evoke a reality too ample for the Portuguese that existed before. Ostensibly a story about magic, this sorcerer's tale is as much about the magic of words as about the assorted magics of the *sertão*.

"São Marcos" is an indirectly confessed fiction, in which Guimarães Rosa subtly reveals the narrator's first name as his own (by allusion to a bird called a *joão-de-barro*) and then elaborates the fiction by informing the reader that in this story his name will be José. The first-person narration begins by recalling several past incidents, but the last part of the tale is recounted largely in the present tense, thus increasing the immediacy of events in the climactic action of the tale.

As is the case with all the stories in *Sagarana*, tone is extremely important in this tale, and the bulk of the narrative is highly entertaining because of the jocular twists of diction and novel lexical forms. "São Marcos" begins with a self-deprecatory recounting of the minor superstitions the narrator subscribes to, by category, ending with the observation that the exact number of superstitions he still holds is seventy-two, evenly divisible by the magic number nine. What he did not believe in at the beginning was sorcery, and he is especially scornful of the recognized master of the local wizards, João Mongolô. He even goes to the extreme of going out of his way to insult Mongolô to his face, a habit which causes his cook no end of anguish, because she and most of the other people in the locale firmly believe in the old man's occult powers. The narrator is so derisive of superstition (except the seventy-two he embraces) that he has the audacity to recite to a friend the diabolical prayer to St. Mark, an especially effective incantation when delivered at the proper time and place and with an appropriate victim in mind.

Numerous magical occurrences, attributable to prayers, assorted magicians, and João Mongolô in particular, are recounted in the opening pages of the tale. At this point the narration is interrupted by a long flashback detailing the narrator's arrival in the village of Fried Lizard and the curious relationship he struck up with the local folk-poets. One day, he tells, he passed a stand of bamboo and noticed a picturesque quatrain inscribed with a jackknife on one of the bamboo stalks. In agreement that the bamboo were asking for decoration, the narrator then carved a challenge on another stalk. Not a poem, but the names of ten ancient Babylonian and Assyrian kings. It is here that Guimarães Rosa interjects his theory of words, noting that they have "song and plumage" and that nature and life have a way of forcing people to stretch the extant lexicon just enough to invoke appropriately the extent of their feelings:

Sargon
Esarhaddon
Ashurbanipal

Tiglath-pileser, Shalmaneser
Nabonidus, Nabopolassar, Nebuchadnezzar
Belshazzar
Sennacherib.

To me this roster of lionly kings, now stripped of their wrathful whims and translated to the realm of poetry, was in itself a poem. Not because of the cylinders of gold and precious stones resting upon the royal waved hair, nor because of the long beards intertwined with threads of gold. Only, only because of the names.

Indeed, aside from their pristine glorious meaning, the whetted blade of those rarely seen and even less rarely heard or used words was priceless to me. For in the presence of an airbrom, a forest molded into an Ionic vase, to say only "treelet" or "heart's rest" is fitting; but on devising, in the midst of the woods, an anjelywood, rearing aloft fifty meters of trunk and foliage, who does not feel the impulse to coin an absurd evocative and shout it aloud—Oh, Colossality—toward the height? (194–95).

Here he begins a correspondence in doggerel with the poet or poets who return during the week to answer his messages, and he confesses that he continues to cultivate this strange art, changing subjects from time to time when one or the other appears to have won a poetic point.

After this aside, and employing the appropriate song and plumage of words, is a long description of the natural surroundings of the area, and the narrator shows himself to be a connoisseur of flora and fauna. Aside from the linguistic pyrotechnics and the poetic control of this passage, it might be thought to be an echo of the descriptivist school, but it is in fact another element important to the climax. For having demonstrated how sharp his eye is, the narrator suddenly goes blind. Though he has a full appreciation of all the senses, his keenest is obviously vision, as the preceding vivid pictorial sketch demonstrates. Now he must use his other senses to get him out of the forest. Though he can in fact recognize most trees by their aroma and texture, he remains hopelessly lost, and finally he shouts out the terrible prayer of St. Mark. At last, frantic and angry, he begins to run, and realizes that he has emerged from the forest into a clearing—in front of Mongolô's shack. He stumbles into the dwelling, tricks Mongolô into speaking, and attacks toward the sound of the voice. Mongolô confesses his guilt and removes the blindfold from the doll he has in his hand, whereupon the narrator's sight returns.

The irony of the tale, though easily visible, is quite complex in the making. Although the theme is superstition, the reader is led to believe that the narrator is very selective about his own superstitions, and indeed he only does add to the list when presented with overwhelming proof. The first sentence of the tale hints at the outcome: "At that time I was living in Fried Lizard, and did not believe in sorcerers" (184). But the reader could hardly be prepared to avoid all the narrative traps, especially since the tale is so consistently entertaining, which tends to lead the reader's attention away from the main story. The other element of extreme importance in the tale is the miniature *ars poetica* included in the section on the bamboo stand, in which Guimarães Rosa reveals his persistent fascination with the power of words and a not altogether innocent delight in constructing worlds out of this interesting material. Freixeiro classifies this story as one of emotional effects and atmosphere,[10] but the various ironies and the denouement leave room for the possibilities of character and idea as well. Most of the irony operates at the expense of the narrator, and the probability of this being a tale of character is reduced by the narrator's hidden identity and by tone, as well as by the lack of real developmental elements of characterization. The only amplification in that sense is that at the end of the story the narrator finally believes in sorcerers. The narrative is too playful by half to deserve classification as a tale of ideas, but there is an important kernel of perception buried in it which may be the theme of the whole book: things not frequently seen and experienced are labeled "magic," and doubted; only occasionally something forces an expansion of the boundaries, and what is considered "real" is a fraction larger than before. This conceit is the analog of the theory of language presented in "São Marcos," since linguistic distension is forced by the inherent deficiencies of the present lexicon. Reading these new linguistic signals is then not dependent on an appreciation of nonsense but on a perception of the sense of the invented forms.

The next tale is almost as magical and just as ironic, and is an even better example of Guimarães Rosa's talent for sustained comic narrative. "Corpo Fechado" ("Bulletproof") opens with a short paragraph about the death of a famous local thug, followed by a dialogue on the subject of thugs between Manuel Fulô and his interlocutor, identified in direct address only as "doctor." The conversation continues for several pages, and bits of information emerge about the town and the characters. The doctor's initial reaction to the town's social life is excruciating boredom, but he has found interest and color in some of the inhabitants, such as Targino, the currently reigning bully, and Manuel Fulô, interesting for being an engaging liar and the only other person in the village who eats mushrooms. The rest of the story unfolds as Manuel and the doctor resume their conversation, this time in a saloon. Manuel is thought to be a Veiga, but now reveals his claim to natural descent from the feared Nhô Peixoto, which makes him heir to courage if not to property. He also has the distinction of being the only person in town familiar enough with Gypsy ways to fool the Gypsies themselves. But he is obsessed by his frustrated dream for a decorated Mexican saddle. The tragic footnote to Manuel's tale is that his friend Tonico has just such a saddle but no mount—Manuel has the animal and no saddle.

This beery conversation is interrupted by the bully Targino, who bursts in to inform Manuel that he has decided to break in Manuel's fiancée on the following day, after which she will return to his care. Advice on what to do comes from all sides, but next morning Manuel has still not decided what to do. At this climatic moment Tonico shows up and has a secret conversation with Manuel. Transformed, Manuel walks into the street to meet his tormentor. He hurls insults at the brute and then attacks him with a small knife he has kept concealed. But five shots are heard. Manuel emerges unscathed but bathed in his victim's blood. Tonico has worked a spell on Manuel which purportedly makes him bulletproof—in exchange for the mule. And all ends well, except that when in his cups Manuel, now the town's tame bully, takes to borrowing the beast, saddle and all, and riding about the town firing a revolver in the air and proclaiming his Peixotesque valor.

Almost a parody of the folktale, "Corpo Fechado" is notable for its comic density and variety, despite the seriousness of the subject matter in the final part. In fact, much of the humor derives from the contrast between tone and content, and the comic and the serious are always in a contrapuntal relationship. Although much of the tale appears to be digressive, as is the case with some other stories in *Sagarana*, the pace here is speeded by the glibness of the main contributor to the dialogue, Manuel Fulô, and by the ironic fluency of the narrator. The alternating points of view and the shifting from dialogue to soliloquy to background narration also contribute to the contradictory character of the tale: single narrative parts have the same leisurely orality and penchant for aside that the folktale often has, but the tale moves rather fast as a whole, especially the last half. Again there are fictions within the fiction, and there are several false starts to the story. The narrator intercedes at least three times to inform the reader-listener that "this is where the story really begins," as if the narrative blocks were separate tales. The last such intercession occurs just before Tonico appears to make Manuel bulletproof, which would make the story itself only a couple of pages long. As in a well-told joke or a well-told folktale, the narrator's observation seems to indicate that a great deal of apparently irrelevant background material must be absorbed to provide the tale with a proper denouement. The punch line itself is not worth much without the various intrigues and suspense established previously, so that process is as important as content.

A number of subthemes which appear in this story have already been seen in others, since much of the tale deals with the arts and sciences of valor, honor, love, envy, deception, and in the end the only solution again turns out to be magic. And again, honor has a price, as do all things. The levels of irony in this tale are complex, but the major dramatic irony centers on Manuel's condition at the end. He not only fails to obtain the coveted saddle, he also loses his beloved mule—but he emerges with both his life and his wife. And he has become, appropriately if ironically, what he has all along demonstrated a talent for: a decorative tough guy.

Freixeiro identifies "Corpo Fechado" as a short story of character,[11] and since the larger ironies and thematic considerations focus on a central character this category is not altogether objectionable, although the revelation of personality is carried out in a rather eccentric form in terms of the short story, and the emphasis on the folk elements gives great importance to place (partly atmosphere, but here more accurately a question of space).

The next tale, "Conversa de Bois" ("Conversation Among Oxen"), is one of the most interesting in *Sagarana*. The narrative root form for this story is most likely the folktale, specifically the fable. All the major characters save one are animals. The tale opens with an unattributed narrative paragraph, in which speculation about animals' capacity for speech is at issue, and the suggestion is made that perhaps such a phenomenon did once exist, but long ago, in the time of the fairy tales. A dialogue follows, in which a certain Manuel Timborna, who is certain that animals can still talk, is pressed by his unnamed interlocutor into telling a story about talking oxen; the interlocutor also asks permission to retell the story, somewhat decorated and expanded here and there. That point agreed upon, Manuel's narrative begins, but a few pages later the reader learns that, not only has the present form of the tale been embellished, but it was originally witnessed firsthand by an *irara* (a grison, a small South American carnivore related to the fisher), which Manuel Timborna captured and agreed to free in exchange for the tale. The unreliability of the narration is thus one of at least fourth degree, since the reader is asked to believe incidents seen by only one witness, a talking animal, retold under duress to a rustic of unknown reliability, and thence conveyed to an anonymous listener with a confessed proclivity for adulterating the data. The last link of this insubstantial chain may or may not be Guimarães Rosa.

This deception perceived, and it is one easily overlooked, the equally deceptive simplicity of the plot unfolds. Much of the perceived reality is that of the oxen, and most of the dialogue is among the eight animals of the team. Each animal is described and characterized by size, color, and disposition. One is foolish, another suffers from indigestion, one is still mourning the recent death of his brother and ex-partner, and each has his physical and psychic idiosyncracies. The oxen share a rudimentary belief system surrounding a "big ox," appear to be aware of a class distinction between themselves and field animals, and unanimously hate men, particularly their driver, Agenor Soronho. To them, he embodies all that is evil, since he mistreats both them and the little boy who guides the team, Tião. They also share anecdotes about an ox called Rodapião, who met an untimely end as a result of his overly logical approach to life.

What appears at first to be the real plot, since this can be taken as just another fanciful setting of scene, is the story of the human characters. The cart is carrying the usual load of sugar plus a less usual cargo, the body of Tião's father, who died that morning. The dead man spent his last years blind and paralyzed, and it appears that during that time Agenor has taken over virtually all the functions of man of the household. Proud and arrogant, Agenor continues to harass both Tião and the team, and when they come upon another cart which has overturned on a difficult slope, he cannot resist the temptation to dramatize his self-importance, and rides to the summit standing on the shaft of his cart. Shortly after the climb, the perceptions of the oxen and those of Tião begin to fuse, and the little boy, walking ahead in tears and only half conscious, starts appearing in the conversations of the oxen as if he were one of them, and finally all of them. The oxen realize how powerful they are, and they also realize that if the detested Agenor, now sleeping, were to fall, he would be crushed under the wheels of the cart. If Tião were to shout, all eight of them would lurch forward, Agenor would fall, and that would be the end. There is a shout and a lurch.

Aside from the complexity of point of view, the story's other principal source of interest is ambiguity. There is a vague allusion to the way Tião's father met his end, since his mother, quite uncharacteristically, cried on discovering him dead, and Agenor, equally uncharacteristically, was gay and expansive. The other plane of ambiguity is that involving the precise sequence of events leading to Agenor's sudden and richly deserved death, since it is impossible to establish a precise sequence of cause and effect. The fused perceptions make Tião and the oxen equally guilty of murder, though only if the reader's already strained disbelief is extended to include communication of a magical nature. Here the suspension of disbelief is, in fact, made more probable by the degree of such suspension already required to accept the implausible chain of narrators through which the tale has passed before reaching its present form.

The story is also one of considerable tension, created through the juxtaposition of antagonistic elements. The most notable of these opposites are good versus evil, animal versus man, and feeling versus logic. Agenor is the antithesis of Rodapião in terms of these tensions. Rodapião met his end for becoming too rational, too much like a man (a frequent motif in the oral folktale), and Agenor met his for being too much the brute (a conceit commonly found in European literatures). The result in both cases is death, the advent of which is morally neutral but inevitable when the balance between human and animal characteristics is lost. The oxen and Tião retain the balance.

Another notable feature of the tale is the use of metaphor and linguistic suggestivity, a major part of the personification of the oxen and an important element of the character fusion at the tale's climax. The oxen, for example, perceive Tião's tears as "slobbering water from his eyes" and the driver as "the man-with-the-long-stick-with-the-hornet-at-the-end" (259). The narrator also describes parts of the oxen with words that in Portuguese are normally used only with reference to the human body, and the oxen frequently refer to themselves with the periphrastic "we," *a gente* ("the people").

The volume's final tale, one of its most famous, is "A Hora e Vez de Augusto Matraga" ("Augusto Matraga's Hour and Turn"), which combines elements of the hero tale and the Holy Bible with the exciting scenario of the better Western movies. A successful Brazilian film has been made with a script based on this story.

The tale concerns a certain Augusto Estêves, who goes by the name of Nhô Augusto (Matraga). Nhô Augusto has one of those exceedingly bad days which Guimarães Rosa found so rich in stories. His wife has left him, his gunslingers have abandoned him, and he is at the brink of financial ruin. Infuriated, he goes after his former gunmen, who beat him to the verge of death, brand him, and toss him over a cliff.

He is rescued by an old Negro couple who lives at the bottom of the canyon, and they slowly nurse him back to health. As his body heals, he resolves that his spirit will do likewise, that he will enter heaven even if he has to do so by force. He becomes a tireless worker and a good Samaritan and gives up all worldly pursuits, including smoking and drinking. News reaches him that his wife is contemplating marriage, that his faithful servant has died in a suicidal attack on Augusto's tormentors, and that his daughter has become a whore. The thought of revenge tempts him, but he does not break his vow to live a holy life.

Another temptation appears one day in the person of the renowned bandit chief Joãozinho Bem-Bem, who offers friendship and a return to the adventurous life as well as the means to carry out revenge. Again, he resists.

Finally sensing that his hour and time are approaching, Augusto sets out alone one day, mounted on a donkey. He reaches a small village and finds Joãozinho and his men about to exact their own revenge on the family of a young man who shot one of the members of the gang. Again, Joãozinho offers Augusto a place in the band, sweetening the offer this time with the bonus of the dead man's handsome weaponry. Aware that the code demands not only the death of the murderer's brothers but also sexual access to the sisters, Augusto reacts in accordance with his new moral code. Having retained the weapons he was looking over, he dispatches three of the bandits—the remaining three flee on seeing the fate of their comrades. Only Joãozinho remains, and the again battered and bloody

Augusto opens his belly with a knife. He insists to the townspeople that they not mistreat the dying bandit and that they give him a decent burial, and he reaffirms his friendship with Joãozinho before the latter expires. Then he dies himself.

"Augusto Matraga" is another confessed fiction, although the confession comes rather tardily, during Augusto's physical and spiritual recuperation, a point at which the reader can be expected to be most committed to wanting the story to be true: "And in this way at least six or six and a half years went by, exactly after this fashion, without adding to or subtracting or deviating from the truth, for this is a made-up story and not something that happened, no indeed" (280). More interesting than the fictional nature of the work, though, are the parallels with the hero tale, and the motifs derived from biblical traditions. There are a number of allusions, some specific and others only vague, to Augusto as a Christ figure, especially at the end, when the inhabitants of the town think him a saint and, not knowing who he is refer to him only as the "Man-on-the-Ass" (302). The structure of the narrative is that of a morality tale, since the exposition, complication, climax, and denouement are thematically arranged according to moral issues. In the exposition, the subject is obviously sin, while in the complication the themes of punishment, repentance, and a gradual return to worldliness are treated. To Augusto, the climax is the point in the tale when he feels his day approaching, which is the day he mounts the donkey and rides off to meet his destiny. The denouement brings the protagonist not only his hour and time, but also salvation, and an unsought popular sainthood. In this context, Joãozinho Bem-Bem is both Satan, with his multiple temptations, and a surrogate victim of Augusto's vengeance.

The similarity of the structure of this story with the old romance of chivalry is also notable, and Fábio Freixeiro may have had this in mind when he classified "Matraga" as a "novela mística."[12] Here, Freixeiro seems to be using the term *novela* not in its pejorative sense of modern popular fiction but in the traditional meaning of early hero narrative, the "mystical" qualifier being added by the demands of the moral inquiry in the tale. This is certainly the most difficult story in the book to classify in terms of single effect, since much of the narrative has the pace of a shoot-em-up Western while maintaining a level of metaphysical speculation and character development excluded from such dramas by necessity. The matter of destiny is also one of overriding importance here, because both the protagonist and the reader know at the outset that the time will come, though neither could have a very clear idea of just how that will take place until the last pages of the tale.

Guimarães Rosa was obviously not the first writer in America to attempt to amplify the confines of regionalism, but time will probably grant him the honor of having done it in an original and inimitable way. Faulkner comes to mind as a comparison, but only again in bits and pieces, perhaps because Faulkner's microcosm was such a stiflling one, perhaps because such comparisons should not be made at all. There is no denying that in Latin America, the "regionalism" of the twenties and thirties and even forties was a thing somehow different from its ancestors, but it was not so very much different. It has not, in fact, changed that much to the present, and talented writers are still able to turn out well-wrought stories of basically traditional assemblage and gain a decent if local reputation by it. In fact, a good deal of "new" fiction is still being produced with the old machinery, as if by changing the label on the machine the resultant product were necessarily transformed, a conceit no doubt Guimarães Rosa would himself have been attracted to.

Most of the Latin Americans, Guimarães Rosa included, have attributed an exalted place of importance to language, as the above label-produces-change example indicates. A matter only lightly touched on in the discussion of *Sagarana*, language is of such importance as to lead critics to talk of nothing else, which if erroneous is at least intriguing. Still, the linguistic novelty of the book is an extremely important source of effect, the feature which most easily identifies the book as a mutation in relation to its predecessors. The previously cited passage on the names of kings and the names of things is a clue to Guimarães Rosa's obsessive love of words. The prose of *Sagarana* is rich in neologisms of several orders, and a number of passages are rendered in rhyme or meter. The following passage, from "The Little Dust-Brown Donkey," is an interesting example.

Flanks swaying, waves of backs rising and falling, tails switching, bellows amidst the wrestling mass, to the rubbing of hide, the crackling of horns, rumbles, thuds, and the fretful lowing of the *junqueira* cattle, with their huge horns, sad and forlorn, homesick for their native fields, the pastures back in the *sertão*. . . .

> Black bull, spotted bull
> Each has his own hue,
> And each heart its own way,
> Its love to prove.

Wild bull, hooking low, slavering slobber, bellowing bull. Dances madly, paws the ground, rushes here, rushes there, right, left. Goes, comes, turns, meets the goad, turns away, turns aside. . . . (20–21)

The translator's admirable attempt to convey both the meaning and the effect is apparent, but something is missing. In Portuguese, the first paragraph, though not versified, is written in verse *(redondilhas menores)*, the second is rhymed, and the third is not only in unmarked verse (these *redondilhas maiores*) but is also composed of three alliterative components, the first with nine repetitions of *b*, the second with ten of *d*, the third with nine of *v*. Also notable, only in part for their linguistic novelty, are such things as the sometimes rhymed bovine catalogs, especially in this tale and in "Conversation Among Oxen," in which the narrator presents a veritable thesaurus of breeds and the likely and unlikely crossbreeds, including descriptions of color, disposition, and origin. There are also observational gems, appalling for their incongruity and accuracy, such as "To make it a rainy day all that was needed was for the water to start coming down. A lowering, sunless morning . . ." (5). In the original the observation is the same, but the morning is a *manhã noiteira,* a "nightish morning," quite impossible in either language. In addition, the prose of *Sagarana* boasts a syntactic inversion on the average of once every six pages, the frequency increasing to one a page in "Matraga."[13] Such emphasis on language might lead to the conclusion that *Sagarana* is either one of the new wave of fun-with-language-for-its-own-sake books, or perhaps just an extension of the down-home school, which delighted in revealing to the world the picturesque folk speech of the natives. *Sagarana* is neither. The use of language is unlike the local colorist tradition in its lack of homeliness and unlike the word-game novel in its purposefulness.

In some senses the modern trend toward playfulness with language has been a means of getting at a larger reality, but it has also been a convenient way to evade the tedious solemnity of the naturalistic approach. That approach, in its regionalist form, tended to bog down both in details of locale and in a kind of bookish prosaicism. Some of the "boom" writers in Latin America have evaded the inevitable by-product of the naturalistic approach, boredom, by scrambling structure, by reproducing in it the chaos of the world, or by manipulating the role of the narrator, with multiple or dead or even nonexistent narrators compensating for anything in the text that might be taken as a symptom of the literal. What can result, unfortunately, is an implied author attitude of superiority, first toward the characters themselves and not infrequently toward the reader.[14] Again, the by-product is likely to be boredom, in part because it is easy to lose the story itself in the process of tinkering with the mechanics of the story. But a good number of the "boom" novels contain a narrator-reader relationship notably similar to the one in *Sagarana*, in which, rather than a magic kindly and condescendingly bestowed, there is a sense of shared wonder. Even when the narrator knowingly withholds information for the appropriate dramatic moment, the process of discovery and pleasure is a mutual one, and Guimarães Rosa's narrators, in whatever guise, exhibit a playfulness finally justified by plot resolution instead of through the rather more gratuitous game of toying with the reader's limited access to truths. It is worth noting in passing that the means by which digression is related to plot, the way information is withheld, and the fluctuations in narrator relation are all generally extracted from the conventions of oral rather than written literature.

Thus the tales in *Sagarana* are openly atavistic in two senses: the narrator and the plot are manifestly important, and the structures employed in the telling of the tales are antiques. What is not at all old-fashioned is something that for lack of a better term might be called "vision," by which is meant an expansion of the fictive at all levels, beginning with language. Unlike the regionalist work of traditional makeup, the tale here is as interesting and enlightening in process as it is in content, though not in the self-indulgent way of novels about the writing of novels or musical comedies about people who make musical comedies or the ultimate banality of movies about the back lot at Warner Brothers. Guimarães Rosa's love for the *sertão* is visible at every turn, but he is never afflicted by the kind of tunnel vision that leads to the production of works dealing with the author's sphere of interest as if it were necessarily the most interesting thing in the world. On the contrary, the tales in *Sagarana* are for the most part as much attempts to discover what might exist as they are descriptions of what exists.

If nothing else, this expanded vision produces a book of tales which prove that the discussion of the short story in terms of "single effect" or even of "active detail" is in modern fiction a chimera. *Sagarana* is at once a "regionalist" work and a "transcendent" one, because the tales, while firmly rooted in the oldest of narrative conventions and able to provide enormous doses of local color, never make that color an end in itself. Thematically the similarity of these stories to those of the regionalist tradition is real but only superficial. The local ethic, the flora and fauna, the idiom are necessary details, but the reader is never left with the arcana as his only reward, and he is never left with the feeling that he has missed the point because he failed to establish residence in the neighborhood. The style of the local raconteur is blended with that of the city-bred and educated (all but one of the tales is told by a thinly disguised Guimarães Rosa, sometimes even identified as an M.D.), and the tone fuses the down-home humor and folk wisdom of the oral teller of tales with the most elaborate pictorial and sonorous effects, erudite references, and literary parallels. There is hardly a character in *Sagarana* not in some degree typical or representative of a rural type, yet there is scarcely a stereotype among them. And as this society is depicted, at the same time a wide-ranging quest is conducted into the spiritual truths of the characters. At last, it is ascertainable that the process of invention itself, so eagerly cultivated by Guimarães Rosa, is perhaps the most accurate way to describe the local reality. The constant viewing of events from a moral perspective, the constant presence of ambiguity and irony, the sharp comic sense, the technical manipulations of language and such features as the contrapuntals (framing devices, tales within tales, even the epigraphs and drawings, the last of which are unfortunately absent from the English translation) are all elements aimed at opening a perspective on a world at once picturesque and startlingly mystical, a world so real it strains credibility.

Guimarães Rosa himself would no doubt have been put off by so ponderous an assessment, since he was one of the few modern writers who did not forget, as many readers and almost all critics appear to have forgotten, that a good tale, well-wrought and enjoyed for the telling and the listening, for the reading, is its own best justification.

CHAPTER 2

# Corpo de Baile:
## *Modes of Comprehension*

THE publication of *Sagarana* in 1946 was an important literary event, introducing to the Brazilian public a new and highly original talent. If João Guimarães Rosa had never written another word, his authorship of this volume of short stories would still have assured him at least a position as one of the great minor Brazilian writers. When a decade of silence was nearing an end, the suspicion that Guimarães Rosa might indeed turn out to be yet another one-shot author began to look more and more likely. In a society with few professional writers, dazzling debuts and writers of perennial but unfulfilled promise are an unfortunate commonplace. Guimarães Rosa, however, had been busy writing during much of that decade, and the results of his labors exceeded the expectations of his most sanguine critics. Not only established at last as an "important writer," Guimarães Rosa became the single standard of excellence in Brazilian prose fiction. The year 1956 thus marks a point at which Brazil's calendar of fiction had its first major revision since Machado de Assis. Henceforth, Brazilian fiction would be either "before Guimarães Rosa" or "after Guimarães Rosa."[1]

The persuasiveness of the evidence was enhanced by the fact that literary history was being rewritten in more than one genre. The first volume to appear was *Corpo de Baile (Corps de Ballet)*, composed of seven colossal narratives which might have been short stories; the second, *Grande Sertão: Veredas (The Devil to Pay in the Backlands)*, was one colossal novel.[2] There was not much doubt that *Grande Sertão*, a book six hundred pages long, fiction, lacking even the space-consuming nicety of chapter divisions, was a novel. There was nothing else to call it, though some were reluctant to use the term. But *Corpo de Baile*, besides being almost too big to tote around in one hand, was also a generic anomaly of sorts. Nobody was really sure what it was, besides difficult.

40

Just what to call the narrative units of *Corpo de Baile* has caused perplexity ever since the volume appeared, and there has yet to emerge a convincing case for any one term. Neither is there any evidence that once such a term can be found its application will provide any better understanding of the effect and importance of the work. The very fact that a mere seven tales originally appeared in two hefty volumes was enough to befuddle most theoreticians, even those who had not read the book. Worse, reading the stories solved nothing. Critics still refer to the narratives as *contos* ("short stories"), *novelas* ("novelettes"), or *romances* ("novels"), often without justifying their preferences, but the term *novela* appears to be the most popular, probably because it is so handily equivocal.

Few Brazilian writers have written fictional pieces comparable to these seven narratives, which accounts in part for the breakdown of the generic terminology. They are several times as long as the ordinary Brazilian short story and longer than a number of books commonly referred to as "novels." Certainly "short story" is an inadequate term if it is meant to suggest the strictly contained microcosmic view often associated with the genre. *Corpo de Baile* has appeared only once in a single volume, in the second edition, released in 1960. In this edition, which was printed on the full-size-page format used for most Brazilian novels, the tales range in length from 43 to 124 pages, the average being 71 pages of small and closely spaced type. In addition to providing more than the usual amount of sheer bulk, Guimarães Rosa made a further backhanded contribution to genre theory by furnishing his own free-floating terminology: the units are listed as seven "novellas" on the title page and "poems" on the following page, but are divided into four "novels" and three "short stories" in the table of contents. One of the "short stories" is thirteen pages longer than the shortest "novel."

English has at least four terms which attempt to describe such mutant fictional forms: two are loan words (novella, novelette) and two are merely alterations (short novel, long short story). All are misleading, because they suggest either hybridization or unverifiable formal distinctions. In addition, the matter of genre, while engrossing, is one of the decidedly minor difficulties involved in an approach to this work.

It would be both imprecise and premature to apply anything but a tentative designation to the narrative units of *Corpo de Baile,* and it is therefore convenient to adopt a name which is at once broad and

formally inexact. One suggestive coinage is Oswaldino Marques'
*prosoema*,[3] which might be rendered as a second definition of
"proem" in English. To avoid the generic and structural implica-
tions of other nomenclature, this term will be used interchangeably
with the word "tale" in reference to these narratives.

The tales of *Corpo de Baile,* besides establishing some kind of
record for length alone, are at the same time composed of some of
the densest stuff in Brazilian literature. Many Brazilians will pri-
vately confess that they wade through the book either with great
difficulty or not at all. Many, even though they may not have read it,
feel constrained to speak publicly in vague but rhapsodic terms
about it. Almost every Brazilian critic worth his salt has written at
least a few lines about the book, but there is nothing in print which
pretends to be a critical introduction, at least none that might prepare the uninitiated reader adequately for a book containing some of
the most "difficult" and at the same time some of the most reward-
ing fictional experiences in modern literature.[4]

It has been suggested, and not in jest, that Guimarães Rosa's
prose can be translated into any language but continental Portuguese.[5] Interestingly, a Portuguese edition of the book is available; at this writing, however, it has not yet been translated into
English, although *Grande Sertão,* longer and certainly as difficult,
has. It is unfortunate but not surprising that *Corpo de Baile* is not
available in English—anything approaching an adequate job would
require the expertise and sense of mission displayed by James L.
Taylor and Harriet de Onís in their translation of *Grande Sertão.*

Clearly the principal reason for the lack of a translation is a linguistic one. That some sort of translation is possible is evidenced by
the Italian and French editions. But Guimarães Rosa's translators
are a rare and dedicated species, lamentably in short supply. And
*Corpo de Baile,* while lacking the subtle difficulties of the highly
elliptical later works, is, with *Grande Sertão,* a book which presents
what appear to be almost insurmountable obstacles to the translator.
Among the works published during the author's life, these two are
not only the longest but also the most obviously experimental in
terms of linguistic deformation. Mary Daniel's excellent linguistic
study demonstrates quantitatively that, although certain categories
of lexical and syntactic experimentation are present in all of
Guimarães Rosa's works, *Corpo de Baile* and *Grande Sertão* stand

out as the two with the most variety and highest frequency of certain experimental forms.[6]

In terms of both difficulty and originality, what was true of *Sagarana* applies doubly, or triply, to this book. A single page of one of these tales is likely to contain enough linguistic novelty to throw the best translator into a state of catalepsy. The first two paragraphs of "Cara-de-Bronze" (345–46), for example, contain at least a dozen neologisms or obscure usages, several ellipses, a number of reverses in word order, and sundry examples of internal rhyme, alliteration, onomatopoeia, and repetition as well as a representative sample of Guimarães Rosa's own inimitable system of punctuation. The page contains in addition an example of typographical alteration, the purposeful double spacing of the word *buritizais* ("fields of buriti palms") as it occurs fifth in a series of six forms of *buriti*. Not a page of the book is free of surprise, hardly a sentence has the ring of a familiar and comfortable cliché. There are few handholds for either reader or translator.

Such exceedingly complex harmonics of language are coupled with elaborate and, for short narratives, massive architectonics in *Corpo de Baile,* the combination likely being responsible for the designation "baroque," which has frequently been applied to Guimarães Rosa's prose. But architecturally, these seven overstuffed tales are as often "Gothic," perhaps even "Romanesque" on occasion. The term here lacks something of the precision vanity demands, and its use may be as misleading as the genre terminology. There is no denying that "baroque proem" is an attractive and tempting possibility, but, although decorative, it seems unlikely to prove very enlightening.

Although "baroque" (kept in quotes) may be a deficient term, it is nonetheless suggestive of some features of *Corpo de Baile* and *Grande Sertão* which differentiate these two works from Guimarães Rosa's others. In literature, the "baroque" style is thought of as a highly ornamented, convoluted style, in which the decorative effect becomes a sort of self-justifying terminus and word play a by-product. It also suggests a philosophical or metaphysical view beyond the play-ethic and beyond words: a view of reality insistently counterpointed by the assumption of an opposite and, distressingly, equal counterreality. Any phenomenon is thus held in the most delicate counterbalance with its nemesis, and the possibility of victories or

defeats is reduced to the utmost unlikelihood. The nearest approach
to Truth is paradox; the fruit of the most dogged investigation is the
ambiguous conclusion. Finally, everything is understandable by
fragments, and all the answers turn out to be correct, but only in
part.[7]

The fluidity of this scheme suggests a hypothesis about "levels of
comprehension" in imaginative literature. Perhaps "modes of comprehension" is better, since the former insinuates a hierarchy of
value, which appears not to be the case with *Corpo de Baile*. What is
meant by the term is merely that this is one of those exceedingly
rich, pluridimensional works, which can be read and reread with a
variety of effect. Most of the signs and most of the symbols may be
taken, correctly, more than one way. Some of them will not even be
taken in their referential or symbolic sense on first reading.

These "modes of comprehension" are produced first by language
in its nuclear form, by sound. Nobody has adequately explained, at
least not in intelligible prose, what effect is produced in the human
imagination by what appears to be a linguistic sign but has no real
"meaning"—much less explained what effect the same sign produces in written form after it is visually apprehended and mentally
produced as sound, soundlessly. It is likewise impossible to explain
with any certainty what kind of *experience* is produced by two lines
of prose containing ten $c$'s [$k$] or by a sentence only sixteen words
long containing seven stressed $a$'s and another fourteen unstressed,
or by a line of prose the reader may not even notice is written in
metric feet.[8] Then there are the bound morphemes, now free. It is
startling to find a form like "ão" sitting all alone as if it were a word,
because its normal use is as an intensifier or as an augmentative
morpheme. It just does not occur alone. But Guimarães Rosa describes a place as "os Gerais do ô e do ão" ("the high plains of oh and
*ão*"), and suddenly it seems that it is no longer a bound morpheme
but an adverb or adjective, perhaps an interjection, potentially even
a proper noun (as, in fact, it is in "Dão-Lalalão"). What matters is
that a signal, however unconventional, has been transmitted and
received and has meaning. A precise close reading of this kind of
text, in which it would be necessary to attribute some definite
meaning to "ão," would result at best in limitation, at worst in
deformation.

The process is even more complicated at succeedingly larger
grammatical categories. The words in Guimarães Rosa's prose may

be agglutinations, back formations, reduplications, or any of a dozen other forms. Most of them are new or arcane words, and again apprehension of meaning in an analytical sense is less important than impressionistic reading, a willingness to accept the new as not only real but necessary. A good dictionary can tell the reader that nobody ever wrote about "alegre relva arrozã" ("happy ricey grass") before, or described a horizon as "azulal" ("like a [cultivated] field of blue"). It cannot diminish the reader's initial surprise on seeing the form, nor dissipate a certain perplexity occasioned by the discovery that the words "don't exist." Since the words, nonexistence aside, are absolutely precise and irreplaceable by existing forms, their plausibility is no longer subject to question. And finally they exist.

Then there is syntax, also new, image, and metaphor, and at last an entire new rhetoric, the poetics of a prodigious reality.

It becomes apparent that diction, in a work so linguistically complex, finally produces a tension of its own. This first mode of comprehension, although apparently external to the work, is still a major part of experience: a tension between content and process. Guimarães Rosa's prose begs the reader's suspension of disbelief to include both. Besides levels or modes of effect (phonologic, morphologic, syntactic), there is a tension apart involving meaning and nonmeaning, so that there exists an omnipresent danger to the reader of being swallowed up in the linguistic process and, finally, mistaking this for the total effect. This tension is comparable in many ways to what is normally regarded as one of the kinds of poetic tension, that constant balancing on the thin edge of revelation. The comparison to poetry is irresistible: the interplay of absolute precision and unintelligibility is a feature of both good and bad poetry. The problem is the temptation to infer a precedence (or substitution) of linguistic experience for the total experience. In the abstract, the idea of reading a story solely for stylistic motives might strike most readers as an unlikely or even obtuse thing to do. But there is some danger of this happening in *Corpo de Baile*: the sensorial and cognitive experience produced by language is so intense that the larger cognitive experience—what else is happening in the story—seems almost superfluous.[9]

Obviously other things do happen in these tales, and somehow Guimarães Rosa has managed to provide here another kind of tension which produces effects as intense as those produced by language. And again, in an unusual way. The short narrative is traditionally so designed that a single aspect of structure at some point becomes identifiable as the central point of tension, the nucleus of conflict. This can be true in novels, although they tend more toward multiple effect; but especially in the short story, the single point of tension is a structural commonplace. It is what used to allow general classifications of short stories into categories such as the short story "of character" or "of emotional effects" or "of atmosphere."

In modern fiction, it has become increasingly difficult to justify these classifications, and Guimarães Rosa is a writer whose contribution to the difficulty is considerable. In general, it could be said that these tales are, with one exception, classifiable as tales "of character." Each tale presents a character or a conflict between characters, an entanglement, and some sort of resolution which produces an illumination of the character or pair of characters. In this sense, the tales are categorizable. But the proems in *Corpo de Baile* also share a structural feature which obviates such easy generalizations. Every proem in the book is like a novel, in that the tale of character is merely the central fragment of structure, a portion of the whole that might be called a "nuclear narrative." Around the nucleus are grouped varying numbers of lateral narratives, ranging in length from a paragraph or two to several pages, and having a relationship to the central core which can at times be perceived only with difficulty. It is here that Guimarães Rosa's classification of the tales as "novels" or "short stories" is in part justified, for in general the "novels" have a higher frequency of subfragments, and generally longer ones.

It is possible, nevertheless, to identify a nuclear narrative in all seven of the tales, and no "short story" is without its several lateral narratives. The proem "Campo Geral" ("Field of the High Plains"), for example, classified by the author as a "novel," has an easily identifiable central narrative thread concerning the coming of age (or coming of awareness) of an eight-year-old boy, Miguilim. The central conflict is that between Miguilim and his cruel father, complicated by Miguilim's internal conflict over the difference between right and wrong, duty and desire. Miguilim's father drives away his wife's first lover, Uncle Terêz, murders the second, Luisaltino, and hangs himself. Shortly thereafter, Terêz, whom Miguilim likes, returns, apparently to take over as head of the family. The final scene in the story has Miguilim being examined by an itinerant doctor, who discovers that the boy is suffering from acute myopia, an affliction which accounts for much of his confusion and clumsiness, as well as explaining to some degree why his father was so short of patience with him.

The surprise ending and the relative simplicity of the plot, in synopsis, suggest a short-story structure of a fairly traditional nature. But interwoven around this central core are numerous sub-fragments, several major characters, long atmospheric passages, even philosophical inquiries. A synopsis of the tale can be written without mention of Miguilim's younger brother Dito, who represents another set of conflicts and whose death provides several moving pages. The nucleus is not affected by leaving out Miguilim's premonitions of death, or his pact with God that he will either die within ten days or survive to live out a healthy life. His affection for the dog Pingo-de-Ouro, the tale of Deográcias and his demented son Patorí, the incident involving the dog Gigão and a bull, a tapir hunt, the frightening and comic episode of the monkeys, a dissertation on good and evil, can all be left out of the synopsis, but the deformation thus produced suggests that the only way to reproduce the tale accurately is completely.

Some contrast is offered by comparing this long narrative to one of the "short stories." In "O Recado do Morro" ("The Message of the Mountain"), the central conflict is based on jealousy. The laborer Pedro Orósio is widely envied for his success with women, and his conquests have naturally earned him the wrath of a number of jealous rivals. One of his rivals, Ivo, accompanies Pedro on an expedition around the interior arranged on behalf of a visiting Danish scientist, but it appears that the two men, instead of fighting, settle their differences and reach some kind of understanding during the trip. Since their relationship has returned to one of a nominally friendly sort, they go out drinking together when the group returns to town. Pedro has picked out a girl for his next conquest, but Ivo insists on taking him to another party, attended only by Ivo and six other former rivals. Almost too late, Pedro realizes what is happening and attacks the seven erstwhile friends before they can kill him, fleeing at last to the safety of his home territory. Again, a fairly straightforward plot, but again several pages could be added to the synopsis without approaching anything like a complete picture. Among the major characters left out are the colorful and at times hilarious Danish scientist Alquiste and a half-dozen bizarre madmen, including one who claims to be working on plans to build an

airplane powered by vultures. Each of these men is the subject of a
lateral narrative. Also tangential are long descriptions of the land,
flora, and fauna. The undercurrent of erotic impulse and the mystery of the mountain are likewise not easily reproduced briefly, so
that what results again is stalemate: it is quite likely impossible to
reduce any of the tales in *Corpo de Baile* to synopsis, because every
fragment is too important to be left out—each is part of a total and
exceedingly complex effect.[10]

Probably the most rational, and certainly the easiest, approach to
the book, then, is on the basis of the individual tale. Many of the
studies written on *Corpo de Baile* deal with only one of the proems
or with a single topic. But there is a consistent preoccupation with
certain elemental forces in all the tales here, and whatever unity the
volume has is discernible through an identification of opposing
energies mentioned with regard to the "baroque" nature of the
work. These energies are of several quite different orders, so that to
consider them "themes" or "motifs" would fall short of the truth. In
the most general sense, in fact, it might be said that all of the tales in
*Corpo de Baile*, while possibly susceptible to categorization as "tales
of character," are a demonstration of Guimarães Rosa's fundamental
reluctance to use easy solutions of any kind. To search for the kind of
"single effect" implied in the traditional classifications of short
stories produces only fragmentary results. All these tales are in
varying degrees "plot" stories and stories "of idea," but since they
are also tales "of character" and "emotional effects" and "atmosphere," it is impossible to justify rationally the selection of only one
of these types as the "single effect." It may be that the effect is one,
but in every case it is an agglutination of several sometimes dissimilar story types: any tale in *Corpo de Baile* can be read as any one of
the five classifications, yet no tale can legitimately be reduced to
only one. "Campo Geral" can be read as a tale of character development, in which Miguilim is at last revealed in epiphany. It can
be read as a plot story, in which events bring about other events—
and in this instance there is a perceivable structure of exposition-
complication-climax-denouement. But it can also be read for the
rich atmosphere, or for ideas or for emotional effects, all of which
abound. The illumination of character is carried out through a process in which plot and atmosphere, important by themselves, are a
vehicle for ideas and emotional effects, which in turn enhance the
former, in a kind of reciprocity of sense. But the basis of this circularity is in a series of moral and thematic considerations not im-

plied by the categories. All effects arise from the pursuit of answers to difficult questions: in this case the following might be enumerated: life versus death, good versus evil, love versus hate, beauty versus ugliness. The specific question of sight versus sightlessness, treated with some irony, involves all the others. Beauty is in the eye of the beholder in "Campo Geral," but the relationship of this idea to other simultaneous ideas and effects disguises and finally belies the facile cliché at first implied.

A handful of such dichotomies provides a manageable if necessarily incomplete system of approach to the seven tales in the book. Some of the more abstract pairs, such as life-death and good-evil, are at least marginally present in all seven. Guimarães Rosa's tales are the product of a mind deeply preoccupied with the essence of things, and the inquiry is conducted in terms of the eternal polar extremes of existence. A frequently meaningless critical commonplace about the author's fiction is its "universal" nature. The term acquires meaning if his tales are viewed from the vantage point of these abstract absolutes.

"Campo Geral" is one of the tales most directly preoccupied with the problem of good versus evil, as demonstrated by Miguilim's serial inquiries:

Dito, how is it that you can know for certain you shouldn't do something, even if nobody else sees you? You know, that's all. . . . Rosa, when do you know that something you're not going to do is wrong? It's when the devil's around. When the devil is near, you can smell the odor of the other flowers. . . . Mother, when you do something, if it's bad, if it's good, how in the world do you tell? Ah, my son, anything you really think is good to do, if you like to do it too much, then you can be sure it's wrong. . . . [Cowboy Jé] What is a bad thing like, so you can be sure? Kids don't need to know that, Miguilim. Kids, when they do something, you can be sure it's wrong. . . . So he asked him [Cowboy Saluz]. How should I know, Miguilim? I never thought about it. I think that when a person's eyes just want to look inside, when he has no need to face others, when he's afraid of wisdom. . . . Then it's wrong. [Dito] Look: now I know, Miguilim. Everything that exists, before it's done, sometimes it's bad; but later when it's done and you did it, then it's good. . . . (43)

Dito's answer, taken by Miguilim in jest, is later clarified: "Evil is mad at both the good and the bad. Goodness is sorry for both the bad and the good. . . . That's the way it is" (57).

The same question, and similar ambiguous answers, recur in various tales in different guises. In "Uma Estória de Amor" ("A Love Story"), the moral question revolves around the dichotomy of sin-virtue, although other oppositions are suggested, such as treachery-loyalty and even solitude-companionship. The ironic title of this tale is an added complication for the reader, who will likely turn the last page and expect yet another, since the love the title implies never materializes. Guimarães Rosa's treatment of love in this story is typical of the tales in the book. Five of the seven tales have a powerful erotic undercurrent, and another ("Cara-de-Bronze") contains a quest motif of an amorous nature. In "Uma Estória de Amor," the aging protagonist, Manuelzão, is beset by the series of conflicting impulses which center on a party he is throwing for the consecration of a small chapel built on the ranch where he works as foreman. His concern with the success of the party is only part of a whole complex of preoccupations about the condition of his life. He worries about his injured foot, which leads him to consider his health in general and finally his mortality. He frets about the cattle drive he is to lead in a few days, which causes him to ruminate about his relationship to his illegitimate son, whom he has brought to work on the ranch with him. In fact, he hopes the son will offer to take the herd to relieve him of such a difficult task at an advanced age, but also because he harbors a consuming desire for his son's wife. His apparent concern about his own success in life is gradually overshadowed by his erotic preoccupations. He recalls his past affairs, speculates about the love life of Joana Xaviel, a mysterious and vaguely deranged storyteller who is attending the party, and finally concludes that for all his apparent prosperity he is as much a failure as the old parasite Camilo.

Although the erotic substratum is only one of several layers of moral speculation here, it is one of the principal sources of dramatic tension in the tale. It is perhaps an exaggeration to speak of dramatic tension in a tale in which so little actually happens, and it is especially difficult to justify the term when, at the tale's end, there is no real resolution. But aside from the linguistic experimentation the clearest source of tension in "Uma Estória de Amor" is the carnal urge.

Two other tales in *Corpo de Baile* are even more directly concerned with the erotic impulse. In both of them the importance of desire is even more transparent than in "Uma Estória de Amor," but at the same time Guimarães Rosa's capacity to abstract essentially primal forces is apparent. In both "A Estória de Lélio e Lina" ("The Story of Lélio and Lina") and "Buriti" ("Buriti [Palm]") the nuclear narratives are based on amorous conflict. In the first tale, the protagonist Lélio signs on as a cowhand at the ranch of a man called Seo Senclér. He is burdened by an unconfessable passion for a wealthy man's daughter, whom he saw only a few times and has idealized beyond reason. The narrative core centers around the avenues of relief for this passion. At first he seeks purely physical relief with a pair of generous freelancers, who provide a free sexual outlet for most of the men in the area. The first real surrogate love he finds evaporates at the touch: she is old Dona Rosalina, who at first appeared to him a young and beautiful girl but turns out to be twice his age. A quasi-saint, Dona Rosalina, her speech larded with pungent aphorisms, subsequently becomes a combination moral proctor and mother confessor to Lélio. Next he betrays a friend by taking advantage of his temporary absence to seduce his hot-blooded mulatta concubine, Jiní. His affair with Jiní is complicated and wildly passionate, and finally ends as violently as it began. The climate in the final half of the tale is one of desperate sexuality, repressed by propriety but emerging in uncontrollable and at times violent ways. Lélio's quiet obsession leads him to consider marrying almost any available female he encounters. He returns for a time to Jiní but separates from her bitterly when he discovers that her chronic infidelity includes him. He returns to the freelancers and even sleeps once with the mysteriously submissive mute girl who lives nearby. The other cowboys, apparently driven by similar passions, are pairing up with the available unmarried females. Finally, Lélio is so lovesick that he seemingly invents a passion for Mariinha, one of the few unclaimed girls. She rejects him, because she too harbors an impossible passion—for the owner of the ranch, Seo Senclér. Lélio realizes he must leave, and at last decides that he will take Dona Rosalina with him.

The curious denouement is consistent with Guimarães Rosa's treatment of love in *Corpo de Baile*. Sexual love is treated not only as a biological urge but as an act of transcendence, a becoming.[11] Desire is treated as a cosmic force, and thus Lélio's affair with Jiní is doomed from the beginning, since it is in this sense incomplete. The tales of *Corpo de Baile* are rife with scandal, betrayal, and passion, at times rendered in the best traditions of erotic literature. A number of the characters in the book are motivated principally by lust, in fact, and thus the interplay between fulfillment and frustration is a major source of tension in tales apparently "about" something altogether different. Guimarães Rosa's treatment of sexuality generally transcends merely libidinous activity, however, as here, and the sexual impulse is often as mysterious as it is powerful. Lélio's decision to take Dona Rosalina with him implies several things about both Lélio and about desire: in choosing understanding and compassion over release, Lélio is also submitting to fate. Dona Rosalina is a living enigma, and her quasi-magical nature as a character suggests symbolic possibilities of both philosophical and mythical dimension. She is a polymorphous being, physically, psychically, and symbolically, so that interpretation of the "meaning" of this final passage necessitates an acceptance of several parallel and probably overlapping layers of signs. It may be that the tale ends with a moral lesson, but if this is so the lesson is one born of enigma.

Repressed sexuality is also important in "Buriti." A kind of humid urgency pervades the atmosphere, recalling the aura of anxiety in Yáñez' *Al filo del agua*. There are allusions to masturbation, lesbianism, exhibitionism, and even rape in this tale, and the characters' quite ordinary daily activities are always suffused with barely controlled passions. The protagonist of the tale is for most of the narrative a minor character, so that what appears in terms of plot to be a love story is structurally an inquiry into the minds of the two main female characters. The nuclear narrative concerns the arrival of a young doctor, Miguel (the Miguilim of "Campo Geral," now grown), to a ranch called Buriti-Bom. The ranch is owned by the priapic old widower Iô Liodoro, who lives with his two daughters and his daughter-in-law, who was abandoned by his son, Irvino. One of the daughters is reputed to be a deranged *beata* ("religious fanatic"), but the other, Maria da Glória, is a beautiful young girl of marriageable age. She and the daughter-in-law, Lalinha, have developed a deep friendship. Miguel is introduced to the family by a neighbor, Nhô Gualberto Gaspar, at whose ranch he stays during his visits. He falls in love with Maria de Glória on his first visit and is eventually fatally drawn back to Buriti-Bom.

In Miguel's absence, Lala and Glória's friendship deepens, and they spend hours talking of men and love. The relationships between characters become increasingly determined by erotic fantasies: Gualberto, a frequent dinner guest, leers at Glória with scarcely concealed lust, Glória confesses to Lala her daydream of appearing at carnival nude but masked, and Lala fans Liodoro's active libido by meeting him secretly at night clad only in a nightgown and having him describe her in erotic detail. The charged atmosphere of sexual tensions finally erupts in a series of incidents: Gualberto assaults Glória one night after dinner and subsequently deflowers her, Lala and Glória comfort each other in something more than sisterly affection, and Lala finally offers herself to Liodoro. Lala prepares to return to town, and Miguel returns at last to claim Glória's hand in marriage.

Though something less than the transcendent force in "Lélio e Lina," the erotic impulse here is nevertheless presented as more abstract than synopsis indicates. Sexual love in "Buriti" is a physical imperative and a moral conundrum. For Glória defloration is part of her destiny as a woman, a destiny she herself sought. She acted as seductress to Gualberto because she believed that Miguel would not return for her. Lala's teasing of Liodoro observes the letter of sexual mores if not their intent, and she offers herself to him in spite: she has ceased to be a member of the family the minute it is learned that Irvino has had a child by another woman. Gualberto, and to some extent Miguel, are unwitting tools in this entangled intrigue. But it is senseless to attempt to distill moral judgments from these tales, because the interplay between biological and spiritual imperatives is always an unresolved conflict. The only clear resolution is carried out by destiny, the most oblique of moral agents.

Guimarães Rosa's preoccupation with essential forces naturally leads to sometimes elaborate inquiries into the matter of fate. More than just a reproduction of the mysterious fatalism of the *sertanejo* mentality, destiny is treated as another of the unknowable elements in the monstrous periodic table of Guimarães Rosa's *sertão*. The characters in *Corpo de Baile* are all in some degree tyrannized by the ubiquity of inevitable outcomes, and the tension produced by their attempts either to thwart fate or to foresee its designs is another of the principal dynamic elements of the book. One tale, reminiscent of "Augusto Matraga" in its preoccupation with the heroic urge and the role of destiny, is "Dão-Lalalão (O Devente)" ("Ding-Ling-a-Ling [Who Owes]"). In one sense a hero tale, "Dão-Lalalão" is also a love story; more so, in fact than "Uma Estória de Amor." The curious title of this tale (in the index the whole title is "Lão-Dalalão [Dão-Lalalão]") remains unexplained in the text of the proem, but is explained elsewhere in the volume: in "A Estória de

Lélio e Lina," Lélio observes that "That's what love was—
lãodalalão—a bell and its pealing" (232). The obscurity of the reference (this clue to the title is buried some sixty pages from the title
page of the tale itself) offers another inkling of the extreme care and
perverse subtlety of much of Guimarães Rosa's prose.

Rather than a theme, destiny in "Dão-Lalalão" is an almost palpa-
ble presence, and this time the reader can foresee with the character (or before the character) the inevitable conflict. The tale's protagonist, Soropita, is the owner of a small store and some land. For
three years he has lived there in relative peace with his lover, the
beautiful Doralda, a retired prostitute. On the way back home from
town one day, he meets with a well-armed group of cowboys, one of
whom is his old friend Dalberto. The etiquette of the *sertão* requires
Soropita to invite Dalberto to his house for the night, though he
immediately fears that there is some possibility that his friend has at
one time slept with Doralda. The thought becomes obsessive, and
his anguish is increased by the thought that one of Dalberto's companions, a muscular Negro named Iládio, may also have knowledge
of his lover. Soropita was for many years a cowboy, and is reputed to
have killed numerous men, so his rational process leads him to the
conclusion that he will be honor bound to kill Dalberto or Iládio if
there is any evidence of what he suspects. His moral dilemma involves love as well as a code of honor, and the difficulty of its
resolution leads him to imagine unthinkable scenes beween Doralda
and Dalberto as justification for what he must do. He questions her
closely when they are alone that night and finally concludes that
they never knew each other. But the image of a Negro customer he
saw in the whorehouse during Doralda's working days haunts him.
When Dalberto's friends come by in the morning, he imagines an
insult on the part of Iládio and sets out armed, to meet his destiny.
The fatal moment arrives when he confronts Iládio and demands
satisfaction, knowing that he will probably die. Surprisingly, Iládio
dismounts and begs for mercy. "Like an evil thought, the Negro
disappeared, for a thousand years. Vultures in the sky devoured the
fame of the Negro" (78).

Unlike "O Recado do Morro," both the reader and the protagonist
sense the necessity for murder and the probability of death early in
the tale. But fate, like everything else in *Corpo de Baile*, is unpredictable, and the whims of destiny are beyond the grasp of presump-
tuous characters and readers alike. And only a rereading confirms

the fact that Guimarães Rosa sowed the seeds of this apparently unlikely turn of events all through the tale.

The vicissitudes of destiny are both obscured and foreshadowed by yet another kind of tension, this one a tension produced by a whole aggregate of elements involving a literal, strictly terrestrial and mortal existence with a mythic and symbolic reality, which seems to parallel and at times to overwhelm the ordinary world. There are symbolic characters and symbolic presences in all these tales, and the extremely intricate mixture of folklore, myth, and symbol is no doubt one of the major difficulties in "understanding" *Corpo de Baile*. This form of tension creates one of the most elusive and at the same time one of the most fertile areas for investigation in Guimarães Rosa, since most elements of the symbolic and mythic reality are, like Dona Rosalina, conscious representations of enigma. Dona Rosalina is simultaneously a protean character endowed with a perceptive power bordering on prescience, an enigmatic love symbol, and a manifestation of characters from a series of folk motifs. Each of these facets of her presence is worthy of more detailed consideration, a fact which obtains with a number of characters and symbols. Another prominent symbol in the book is the buriti palm, which, aside from its obvious phallic connotation (amply explored in "Buriti"), has an important symbolic potential in a number of tales. In some cases the buriti is clearly a symbol of life and vitality, but at times (as on the first page of "Cara-de-Bronze," cited above) it has a magical and not precisely identifiable role. More than just a piece of personified vegetation, the buriti at times assumes the importance of a mysterious elemental energy. "The buriti is the palm of God! " (160) is a phrase which hints at only one aspect of the tree's significance.[12]

There are so many obscure symbols and so great a quantity of mythemes and folk motifs that only a very few can be mentioned. It is not likely that a full catalog, much less a complete study, is possible, or even desirable, since the impossibility of establishing one-to-one relationships in *Corpo de Baile* is a principal source of the book's art. There are enchanted cattle and enchanted cowboys, cabalistic numbers (three and seven are very frequent), flight motifs, witches, and magic spells. At times such elements appear to be nothing more than decoration, but even when they are not foreshadowings (as in "O Recado de Morro")[13] they are part of the necessarily complex totality of effect.

One of the most interesting characters in the book is the mysterious personage who provides the title for the proem "Cara-de-Bronze" ("Bronze Face"). This tale is the least conventional and one of the most difficult in *Corpo de Baile*. Written as a cinematic script, complete with stage and lighting directions, "Cara-de-Bronze" is also the only story in the volume which employs footnotes, yet another example of Guimarães Rosa's obstinate originality. How the footnotes would be incorporated into a screen version is not explained.[14]

The scene is Cara-de-Bronze's ranch, where a number of people have gathered for a cattle sale. The first scene consists of a complex dialogue between the cowboys of other ranches and those who work for Cara-de-Bronze. Speculation centers around just who Cara-de-Bronze is, what his real name is, and what could have been the mysterious nature of the two-year quest from which Grivo, one of his cowhands, has just returned. The tale contains one of the clearest examples of the importance of names:

Iinho Ti: Bronze-Face. Those are nicknames. . .
Cowboy Cicica: "Senior" isn't a nickname, it's a legal name.
Cowboy Adino: Name's Sigisbé. Cowboy Mainarte: Sejisbel Saturnim. . .
Cowboy Cicica: Xezisbéo Saturnim, for sure. But "Senior" as well. "Senior" isn't just a handle—it's a surname. . . Cowboy Sacramento: Man, I don't know. As far as I've known, forever, it's just Jizisbéu. . .
Cowboy Doim: Zijisbéu Saturnim. . . Cowboy Sacramento: Jizisbéu Saturnim, I think. (349)

And on the following page:

Cowboy Adino: Papa Tadeu, how do you reconcile the old man's name, completely, registrally?
Cowboy Sãos: Sezisbério . . .
Cowboy Tadeu: Why, hey, you guys? Name of the man, all of it?
Cowboy Cicica: However it may be, as if I were to ask for it, compadre Tadeu.
Cowboy Tadeu: His name? Well, then: Segisberto Saturnino Jéia Senior, Junior—the way he signs it at the bottom of documents.

And finally, "Cowboy Tadeu: Now, the 'Junior,' he himself puts and takes: with his own hand, then he crosses it out . . ." (350).
Namer-as-maker apparently touches even the lowliest cowboys: a

person or thing can only be apprehended in the mind with any accuracy if the correct name is given. It is not at all unlikely that things and people take on a different configuration when called by a different name, or when a name is examined for its occult meaning. Paulo Rónai has noted, for example, that Guimarães Rosa himself appears as a character in this tale—in the guise of a man called Moimeichêgo, whose name is an agglutinate of personal pronouns in four languages: "moi," "me," "ich," "ego." [15] A similar naming / configuration item occurs in "Dão-Lalalão," where Soropita is terrifying to the other cowboys at least in part because to them his name is "Surrupita." Even Doralda seems to have alternate names for different faces of her femininity: "Sucena," when she was still a prostitute, now Doralda (Adoralda) or Dola or Dadã or even Môça Branca as faces of her present personality, declensions of tenderness and sensuality. [16] There are a number of other characters in *Corpo de Baile* who have alternate names, especially in "O Recado do Morro," but even those with only one name are somehow given a particular configuration by the suggestivity of the name, such as Adelco de Tal ("Adelco So-and-So"), the nonentity-son in "Uma Estória de Amor," or even little Miguilim ("Mikey").

Cara-de-Bronze, even when his name is finally established, is a mysterious and amorphous character. His age and health are matters of considerable speculation. Even his complexion is the subject of debate, and it is finally resolved that he can be described as having "dusky pallor," that he is dark but was formerly darker. He may be crippled or paralyzed, it is said that he loves trees, and in the second scene it is revealed that he may have leprosy. There is no agreement whatsoever about his moral character, and he seems to embody so many contradictory characteristics that it is impossible for the cowboys, and finally for the reader, to determine just what kind of person he is. In the second scene the rumor of Grivo's marriage is confirmed, and at this point the author intervenes to inform the reader that the story is not really about Cara-de-Bronze nor about Grivo, but about the girl he brought back from his quest, "the Very-White-One-of-All-Colors." Grivo finally comes out on the porch and starts to tell of the beauties and perils of the journey. He is called in to see the old man briefly, returning shortly thereafter to tell at last that what he saw on his journey was "all there is." The old man has asked him to describe a bride's hammock and he has complied. Cara-de-Bronze finally asks for Grivo's blessing and then be-

gins to cry, and the cowboys now speculate that Grivo will inherit
some of Segisberto's land. The tale ends with one of the cowboys
outside "listening to the thirst of the cattle."

Interspersed into this curious narrative are the footnotes, which
range in apparent relevance from the shouts of men on a cattle drive
to quotations from the *Upanishads*, and in length from a few lines to
a whole catalog of fauna (some 60 items) and flora (almost 400
items, with *buriti* in caps). These asides are of little or no immediate
help in unraveling the mysteries of the tale. They are one of the
most clearly identifiable "baroque" features of *Corpo de Baile*, as
they are intimately connected with the magic of names just discussed in relation to people. They can be read for scientific interest,
for their sonorous impact, as a treatise on the picturesque features
of *sertanejo* nomenclature, or not read at all, although they have a real
structural function, if a somewhat obscure one. The bulk of the
footnotes constitute a kind of substantive synopsis of Grivo's quest,
suggesting not only his isolation from human contact, but also the
length and difficulty of the journey. There is also a note of wonder
provided, especially by the footnote on plants, and finally it must be
noted that these catalogs not only contribute background and atmosphere but also serve to give a perspective on a universe inhabited by a seemingly infinite number of things. Like our own,
Guimarães Rosa's universe is a singular and eminently confusing
place to live in—what may appear to be gratuitous decoration is
really part of an ontology of that universe: everything depends on
knowing the universe, and a familiarity with the things that make it
up is imperative. To know the precise name of a thing is to know the
thing, and each known thing is another fragment of the known
universe.[17]

Another important part of this system of knowing provides the
final kind of tension to be discussed here. In the most general sense,
it arises from the polar extremes of madness and sanity, but like
other extremes the poles may appear in a circular relationship rather
than in a linear opposition. This tension is the most obvious in "O
Recado do Morro," in which there are five characters of varying
degrees of madness. As is so often the case, most of these characters
have alternate and highly depictive names: Gorgulho (Malaquias),
Catraz (Cualhacôco), the goitered idiot Guégue, Jubileu (Santos-
Óleos, or, astoundingly, Nôminedômine), the Collector. The mad
characters in this tale have a clear function as prophets. As Maurice

Capovilla has noted, there are two isolated planes of reality in "O Recado do Morro," one of madness and one of sanity. The "message" (the premonition, based on myth, that Pedro Orósio's seven friends will attack him) is carried from one madman to another, then to a child, and finally to a singer (or, as Capovilla observes, a *minnesinger*), who repeats the message in song and at last transmits the message to the protagonist.[18] Again, there are cabalistic numbers (the message is transmitted seven times, the treachery involves seven rivals) and involved fusions of myth and fact. What is important is the role of the message bearers: five madmen, one child, one poet.

These and similar characters abound in *Corpo de Baile*. In addition to characters clearly identified as madmen, there are numerous other personages perhaps best described as "marginals," and who, like poets and children, have access to hidden or occult information. In some cases they are used as vehicles for foreshadowings, as in "O Recado do Morro," but at times they are relatively static but nevertheless mysterious beings, often suffering from physical as well as mental afflictions, such as Cara-de-Bronze (possibly a leper) or the blind man with a perfect memory for voices in "Dão-Lalalão." Every tale in the book has at least one such character, although they are pivotal figures in only three of the tales.

In "Uma Estória de Amor" there is a madman, João Urúgem, who seems to be a homologue of Gorgulho, in "O Recado do Morro." Both are pariahs who, for unknown reasons, live in caves, surrounded by vultures. But João Urúgem is less important as a prophet than Gorgulho: the foreshadowing in "Uma Estória de Amor" is carried out by the possibly demented and oddly erotic Joana Xaviel, a storyteller, and by old Camilo, himself decrepit and somewhere beyond senility. Joana Xaviel's unfinished tale in fact foreshadows the muted ending of "Uma Estória de Amor," because the reaction of the major characters is that no tale can end in the air like that—there must be more. The reader may share this feeling on finishing the proem.

There are also several highly eccentric or definitely deranged characters in "Buriti," although their function is less one of prophecy than as contributors to the atmosphere of anxiety. The most interesting madman in "Buriti" is "Boss Zequiel," who babbles senselessly through the tale until the day Maria da Glória's sister, Maria Behú (the *beata*), dies, whereupon he returns to sanity.

Although the bridge between madness and sanity is at times traversed, prophetic vision of several kinds is an insistent counterpoint to a lesser view of reality. And even in tales in which disease and eccentricity are the closest approaches to madness, as in "Cara-de-Bronze," the task of foreshadowing and counterpointing is given to another marginal, the poet-singer.

This discussion of "modes of comprehension," viewed as the product of various kinds of tension, is admittedly a partial one. One of the features of *Corpo de Baile* not discussed in any detail is the question of "unity." In this case the question is not a particularly important one, but it is worth noting that all the kinds of tension discussed are general and parallel and occur throughout the volume. There are a number of other considerations which could be mentioned in this context, including the obvious matter of repeated characters. Miguilim, for example, is the protagonist of both "Campo Geral" and (as an adult) "Buriti," respectively the first and last tales in the book. He is also mentioned, and his siblings are characters, in "Lélio e Lina." Grivo and Cara-de-Bronze also appear in at least two tales, and others, probably in disguise, may appear more than once as well.

Some of the traditional topics of approach, such as characterization, time, and space have not been dealt with here—not because these matters are unimportant or outmoded, but because they are handled in what must still be qualified as only a "relatively" traditional manner. One key feature of characterization is the conscientious use of given names and nicknames as fundamental clues to physiognomy and character.[19] Time is also an extremely important element in the tales of this volume: in "Dão-Lalalão" there are scenes which occupy only seconds of chronological time but may take pages to set forth because of the importance of psychological time.[20] "Buriti" has some intriguing temporal features as well, including very extended flashbacks and parenthetical descriptive passages which evoke, with the fine touch of poetry, such events as the fall of a single palm leaf in an uninhabited forest. Space is also managed with great care. These two elements, time and space, are, in fact, further substantiations of Guimarães Rosa's division of the tales into "novels" and "short stories." Although not precise by the classic standards, time and space are relatively limited in the short stories, complex and extensive in the novels. Even point of view deserves further consideration, because although all the tales save

"Buriti" are apparently third-person omniscient narrations, there are considerable modifications. Aside from the case of the hidden narrator in "Cara-de-Bronze," one of the most interesting of these is in the tale "Campo Geral," in which the reader's epiphany coincides with Miguilim's, because the bulk of the narrative is so closely related to the character's hazy view of things that the technicality of omniscient narration is made irrelevant: the reader cannot until that point know that Miguilim is practically blind because Miguilim himself does not know it.

*Corpo de Baile* is not an "open" work in the current acceptation of forcing the reader into a participant role in the fictional process, but it is a volume which provokes a high degree of reader involvement, because it is so confected as to invite multiple and even contradictory responses. The admittedly incomplete approach suggested here is merely one of a number of legitimate ways of dealing with the frequently baffling "baroque" narratives of *Corpo de Baile*.

As in all of Guimarães Rosa's works, it is linguistically so opulent as to tempt satisfaction from idiom alone, but (paradoxically, in a work so inventive in this area) language remains a vehicle for dramatic effect rather than a replacement. The tales of *Corpo de Baile*, distilled to nuclear form, are in some senses reducible to fairly conventional categories, as long as that reduction is taken as a conscious deformation for the purpose of edification. Thus reduced, it becomes apparent that altogether too much has been left out, that an obstinate author has taken advantage of our faith in nomenclature. The categories overlap and even substitute for one another.

Since most of the conventional tools fail, it has been suggested that one way of seeing past the ornamentation without losing the essence is to view the tales as a series of inquiries into a number of universal questions. The questions can be taken, and interpreted, in various ways: philosophically, theologically, sociologically, dramatically, poetically. But they are the same questions regardless of which sectarian interest the reader chooses to adopt in the interpretation.

These questions are all posed through forms of tension, and each seems to substantiate both the much abused assumption of "universality" as it provides yet another clue to the unity of the volume. The base elements of conflict in *Corpo de Baile* are part of the stock of timeless interrogations of Western literature: life and death, sin and virtue, good and evil, free will and destiny, madness and sanity. In the process of inquiry a baffling array of symbols, mythemes, and folk motifs is employed, not always in ways that are likely to satisfy wholly the reader whose cultural tradition emphasizes a sense of precision. The cast of characters includes cowboys with metaphysical anxieties, aged sex symbols, holy idiots, and blind prophets, even trees and animals. Characters and scenes and climaxes and symbols are obstinately polyvalent, to the point that a character cannot be trusted to have the same name throughout the tale.

What can be and must be said is that the one thing *Corpo de Baile* will provide any reader is surprise. Surprise is present from the most elemental linguistic fragment, sound, through the most sophisticated of philosophical mazes. The reader may experience moments of recognition anywhere from a striking parallel to an unsayable revelation to the vaguest of echoes. Effect, however, is produced not cognitively, at least not in a cognitive process easily reduced to exegesis, but by resonances. And resonance is a subtle and elusive nonthing, which varies immeasurably from reader to reader, from reading to reading.

It never quite ceases to be somewhat confusing. It is also a delight to read, occasionally intimidating, and in its own perverse way enlightening beyond the range of most books. Finally, although it is hard to lay a hand on exactly what must be said about it, it is impossible to resist the temptation to explain, to interpret. Then, like Grivo, after naming his four hundred plants:

*"Is that all there is?"*
"A lot has been left out. Almost everything has been left out." (375)

### CHAPTER 3

# Grande Sertão: Veredas:
## *The Critical Imperative*

*G*rande Sertão: Veredas, translated into English with the misleadingly banal title of *The Devil to Pay in the Backlands*,[1] will
unquestionably stand as one of the monuments of twentieth-century
Brazilian literature. Even if critics were somehow persuaded to call
a ten-year moratorium on publishing articles about it, as some have
suggested not altogether in jest, the extant bibliography would still
probably constitute a record for commentaries on a single volume of
Brazilian fiction, both numerically and in terms of bulk. No one has
attempted to explain the reasons for the relative paucity of studies
on Guimarães Rosa's other works, but certainly one of the attrac-
tions of this lone novel is its suggestive range: a comparative-litera-
ture specialist's dream, GSV has inspired an extraordinary wealth of
interpretations of every description, both in Brazil and elsewhere,
and it is no longer likely that any single critic has a scholar's command of the literature on the subject.

Such a book must be approached with caution, and simple prudence dictates that matters should be left as they are. But, as any
missionary knows, prudence is easily overcome by an abundance of
zeal. There is not yet any indication that the flood of studies is about
to abate. Almost every critic who has written on the subject has
somewhere along the line established a comparative base as an initial foothold, in some cases as praise by association; more often
because the book seems to demand that a context be erected around
it before things make much sense. The attractiveness of analogical
statements is particularly strong because of the very difficulty in
making good ones, since virtually all of them can be proved falla-
cious on one basis or another, yet a comparison—a classification—is
the easiest rational means for constituting an approach to the novel.

Most of the comparisons made to date are not limited to analogy with a single work, though the general tendency appears to be the selection of the monumental works of world literature.[2] Since *GSV* is a work of relatively recent vintage, it is worth considering a framework both modern and accessible to the English-speaking reader. The risks of absurdity and inaccuracy accepted, it might be hazarded that of modern works in English, two very dissimilar but illustrative contemporary monuments would be Pynchon's *Gravity's Rainbow* and Tolkien's *Lord of the Rings* trilogy. If nothing else, this parallel suggests something about the scope of the book. The comparison is not altogether pointless, however. Though it would be difficult to find very precise thematic or stylistic reasons for the analogy, *GSV* occupies in Luso-Brazilian literature a position which is close to being a composite of the positions of these two works in the recent fiction of the English-speaking world. It shares with *Gravity's Rainbow* the ambition of inclusiveness and a sense of termination. Like Pynchon's work, it is an attempt to explain the world. The attempt is made in the pursuit of rules, in a place where rules defy explanation. Like the *Lord of the Rings*, it is in many ways blatantly archaic, and it achieves effect in large measure through an appeal to what was once called "cultural memory," a complex set of stimuli designed to provide subverbal but often quite specific responses in the reader. Like both these books, *GSV* is also a cult novel, because reactions to it are of an order that allows no middle ground. There is no empirical test to predict how intelligent and cultured people will react to any of these novels: the alternatives appear to be fanaticism or militant disinterest, depending upon whether or not the reader's chords of recognition and response are struck.

In Brazil, *GSV* was welcomed with a rush of critical praise that is still unequaled, tempered only by a few cautious remarks about its unintelligibility, provoked, it would seem, by an unstated suspicion that the thing just might have been a fraud, concocted by some editorial committee to bamboozle those too awed to perceive the trick. Others recognized the real merits of the book but had reservations about what this impressive but nevertheless very white elephant might do to national letters. Adolfo Casais Monteiro called *GSV* a "monster," and, comparing its probable position to that of Joyce's *Ulysses* in the English-speaking world, speculated that, like *Ulysses*, it could some day come to be regarded as a sort of literary roadblock, "tying up traffic," as a work of great importance but perennial exception.[3] The literary establishment was nevertheless too impressed to allow any such metaphors of transit to discourage the recognition it thought the novel deserved. The Brazilian National Book Institute gathered its critics together the year the work was published to decide which of the many works of fiction published that year deserved the "Prêmio Machado de Assis," comparable to the U.S. National Book Award. In an almost unprecedented display of harmony, the prize was unanimously awarded to *GSV*.[4] Since that time, the book has been the recipient of some of the most lavish acclaim ever afforded a single work in Brazil, and it even became a standard topic at gatherings of the literary chic, many of whom must have been annoyed by the critics for not being more specific about the book's "real meaning." A search for that real meaning can and should lead the critic down a number of paths of all shapes and sizes. The "critical imperative" alluded to in the title of this chapter is that, in the process, it is a good idea to be careful.

A novel provoking responses ranging all the way from the most complete disorientation to the most ecstatic accolade might be thought to be one of those vast, disjointed, and anarchic affairs which the modern novel has in some senses become, the sort of book that only half succeeds at a dozen things because it ambitions everything. *GSV*, while not in diametric opposition to that description, is, for a multivalent work, extraordinarily controlled. Though it lacks the facile linearity of the realistic novel, there is never any sense that the author's material has gotten the best of him. And, at least on a superficial first reading, it might be taken as an only somewhat jumbled plot, in fact, a cowboy story.

The action is presented as a fictional interlocutor spends three days listening to the autobiographical account of several years in the life of the narrator. Though the interlocutor's speech is not registered, the narrator reacts to whatever he does say. The narrator's name, Riobaldo, is not revealed until page 32. Riobaldo reveals himself and the plot through his two major preoccupations, both of them so obsessive as to appear pathological, both framed as questions: one concerns the existence or nonexistence of the devil, the other concerns the equally equivocal relationship Riobaldo had with a fellow bandit named Diadorim. Chronologically, the story begins during Riobaldo's youth and carries him to his present advanced age. Riobaldo meets Diadorim as a young boy and later encounters him again after he has begun a career as a *jagunço* (a gunslinger belonging to a band in the hire of a politico). Episodes of varying length detail the circumstances which led him into this kind of life, his love affair with a prostitute, and his more romantic attachment to a girl called Otacília, but the principal focus is on the involved and lengthy war between rival bandit groups. The sequence of dramatic events begins with the death by treachery of the great bandit chieftain Joca Ramiro, who is replaced by Medeiro Vaz. Medeiro Vaz resolves to impose justice by force of arms but is felled by disease, to be replaced by the interim chieftain Marcelino Pampa. The ferocious Zé Bebelo, the former rival chieftain with whom Riobaldo began his career, then comes out of exile to avenge Joca Ramiro's death. He is finally replaced by Riobaldo, whose name becomes Urutu-Branco (White Rattlesnake) on his assumption of the band's leadership. Through all these changes of leadership and allegiance, the principal aim of the protagonists is to destroy the traitors Ricardão and Hermógenes, the latter of whom is reputed to have entered into a pact with the devil. As a countermeasure, Riobaldo alternately suggests and denies, he himself may likewise have made an agreement with Satan to guarantee the success of his endeavor. And throughout the narration, Riobaldo elaborates on the disturbing and fascinating relationship he developed with Diadorim. Finally, Riobaldo leads his men across the forbidding Sussuarão Desert, where they destroy Hermógenes' ranch and capture his wife. The climactic battle scene begins with another sneak attack. Riobaldo is sharpshooting from the roof of a building, when suddenly the two rival gangs on the ground line up and charge in the open. Diadorim kills Hermógenes and dies in the act. Shortly thereafter Riobaldo's prisoner (Hermógenes' wife) is preparing the beloved friend's corpse for burial, and she finally reveals to Riobaldo what has been hinted at all along—Diadorim was really a beautiful young woman, pledged to struggle in male disguise until avenging the death of her father, Joca Ramiro. Riobaldo's view of these events, seen in the perspective of hindsight, is by turns ironic, pathetic, and dramatic. Riobaldo has retired from banditry to the comfort of an inherited estate, married Otacília, and settled down to a life of relative ease. But as his narrative demonstrates, he is not yet really at peace, and his memory continually provokes him into attempts to clarify the past, to explain the world.

The reader is not likely to emerge with such a synopsis until very near the end of the book, if indeed he could construct one at all on a first reading, and here is one of the infrequent occasions when theories of the novel can be useful to other than theorists themselves. Meir Sternberg derives from Russian Formalist critics the distinction between *fabula* (roughly speaking, the chronological or causal sequence in which the motifs of a story occur) and *sujet* (again only generally, the disposition of these same motifs in the hands of the artist, the order in which things happen in the work itself, and the way in which they are conveyed).[5] In the above synopsis, only fragments of the *fabula* have been related; the *sujet* remains without comment. A traditional tool for the explication of the "other" elements has been a discussion of "point of view," but here the variables are so numerous and in such complex interrelationship that an examination of point of view as an isolated element of narrative construction is futile. What is important is not only the relationship of *fabula* to *sujet* but also the relationships among reader, narrator, interlocutor, and perhaps author as well, all of which can be discussed under the umbrella of "rhetorical design."

Critics are far from unanimous about how to characterize the expository process in *GSV*, but most are willing to admit that it only appears to be monologue. Because of the indicated presence of an interlocutor, the limitations and potentials of monologue are avoided, but since the speech of this fictitious interlocutor can only be conjectured, the narration is not yet dialogue but half a dialogue, or solipsistic dialogue.[6] The rhetorical model is one familiar to Brazilians, but it is complicated by, among other things, the medium in which it is presented. Magazines and newspapers in Brazil frequently publish interviews with rustic old characters like Riobaldo, but although the interlocutor here is a man of letters, takes notes, and presumably records accurately what is being said, it is important to consider not only the fictitious natures of the speaker and the recorder but the artificial orality of the "speech" as well, since no known individual actually talks as Riobaldo does.[7] First-person narrative by its very nature presents the reader with one of the fundamental problems of disbelief, since the reader is at the outset aware that a selective process is at work in the ordering of events, in the interpretation of data, and in the emphasis given to one fact (or lie) over another. In *GSV* the selective process is even more apparent, because not only are things told out of chronological order, they are confessedly given greater or lesser emphasis not in regard to any inherent historical importance they might have had but depending on what kind of effect they had and continue to have on a narrator who only occasionally reminds the reader that his own view vacillates. This is perhaps to be assumed along with other assumptions about this kind of narration, but here the predominance of interpretation over fact and the constant fluctuations between represented time (the duration of a period in the life of the character) and representational time (the time it takes the reader to absorb the information about that period)[8] give the narrator an almost tyrannical control over the reader's channels of information. Of equal importance is the interplay between past and present, though in GSV there is a constant in the evaluative posture of the narrator. One narrative plane is the present, half dialogue, in which the narrator evaluates what happened in the past, what is happening in his present life, and the act of narrating itself; a second plane is past, in indirect discourse, in which the action takes place.[9] These two planes intersect and are framed in random or affective order, and thus the book is filled with dozens of "expositions" and scores of temporal dislocations. According to Antônio Cândido, this process reduces the past, which is the bulk of the narrative, to a sort of appendix to the present,[10] because the narrator is in a constant state of inquiry concerning everything that happens or might have happened. The narrator's position is at best a slippery one, because the reader tends to forget his proximity to Riobaldo during the long historical sections, at least until he returns to make yet another present-related question out of the past.

But what about the interlocutor? Though he presumably speaks, the reader knows only by inference what he says, even though his opinions are frequently solicited. The interlocutor may be described as a "haunted listener,"[11] but this position in a kind of fictive limbo applies to the reader as well. Since the reader is necessarily (to be reading the book) a person of letters and the principal receptor of signals, his identification with the interlocutor is strengthened by means of what might be termed a rhetorical trap. The reader is also led into closer identification with Riobaldo through this scheme. In addition, Riobaldo's continual appeals for assistance in completing the story or in discerning the truth or falsehood of events, along with the chronological device of returning unexpectedly to the immediate fictive present vastly modify the traditional reader-narrator-character relationship. Antônio Cândido has observed that one of the book's strengths is the fact that *jagunços* in other novels are sympathetic but not empathic, while the reader feels that he *is* Riobaldo because he is perpetually facing problems common to humanity.[12] Reader identification is thus thematic and philosophical, but it is also reinforced by a complex rhetorical design which eventually leads the reader into a very close association with the making of the fiction. It is unlikely that readers have ever been so naive as to overlook totally the illusions being constructed by novelists, but *GSV* requires the reader to relate to the text in so many ways that his awareness of identifications and participation is considerably diluted. Technically, the reader can only be a reader, but he is relating to the narrative as the recipient of an unknown person's version of things, and the narrator is retelling a story in which he was the main character. The narrator confesses that parts of his tale may not be true, and there are several hints that the interlocutor is also the author. To follow the story, the reader must also participate to some degree in all these roles. Finally, it should be noted that the reader is not supposed to be reading the story at all, but listening to it, yet another of the several veils which simultaneously conceal and enhance the fiction.[13]

Aside from this design, the other major stumbling block to an intelligent reading of the novel is language, a feature which has generated a preponderance of the studies on the work. *Sagarana* inspired surprise on this issue and *Corpo de Baile* no less than awe, but none of Guimarães Rosa's works has yet provoked such fervor as *GSV*. The narration of *GSV* is a rambling, chapterless treatise on life and the world, rendered in a gnomic style that combines the characteristics of a fanciful rural Brazilian speech and world view with some equally improbable elements of a likewise nonexistent erudite diction. The processes of linguistic change are the same ones noted in the two earlier works, though *GSV* has a higher incidence of syntactic inversions (two per page) and "future phonology" (imitation of a phonological process already under way to anticipate future words).[14] Among the high frequency forms found in *GSV* are Latinisms, Indianisms, expletives, pleonasms, and assorted morphological deformations, most of which are derived from the analogical processes already at work in Portuguese.[15] The analogical process is a somewhat more sophisticated version of the logical steps a child might take to form the word "foxen" on the basis of his knowledge of the irregular "ox-oxen," or to coin "oxes" on the assumption of noun plural regularity. Wilson Martins criticized *GSV* in one of his earlier studies for being so reliant on such stylistic quirks, especially since the style corresponded to no sociological reality and was at odds with some "fundamental rules of composition."[16] Others simply refuse to read the novel because it appears to be written in an invented language. Whatever shape reader reaction takes, it is clear that style in this work is of such overriding importance that it must be considered part of the *sujet:* the achronological disposition of motifs is supported, or complicated, by the seeming illogic or unreality of diction, and the reader necessarily responds to the manner signals are conveyed simultaneous with his reaction to their ordering. This is not to say that the language is simply a frivolous invention. Guimarães Rosa's coinages are legitimately compared to those of Lewis Carroll, because there is an underlying logic in the process which may—and generally does—cause the native speaker to respond, though he may do so *analytically* only if he wishes to explain his reactions to a third party. Often it is impossible to be certain whether words and expressions used in the novel are regionalisms or inventions, but it is generally conceded that Brazilians find the work difficult or even impossible to read because of its linguistic deformities.[17]

When Riobaldo interrupts his historical narrative to comment on the difficulty of telling, he is not only commenting on the story itself but on the fluidity of the system of signals established in his narration:

> One keeps the memories of his life in different compartments, each with its own symbols and sentiments, and I don't think they mix with one another. You can only relate things straight through, one basted to the other, when they are matters of minor import. (81)

> Many important things have no name. (91)

> What is a name? A name does not give; a name receives. (132)

> Ah, but I am not telling the truth. Do you sense it? Telling something is a very, very difficult business. Not because of the years that have gone by, but because certain things of the past have a way of changing about, switching places. Was what I have said true? It was. But did it happen? Now I'm not so sure. (154)

Riobaldo's attitude toward his material is one of both wonder and urgency: he appears compelled to admit the probable inaccuracy of what he tells but determined to tell it, as if in the telling some sense of the real truth might emerge. There is something of the attitude of the mystic in this posture, which is one reason that even the best analyses are limited to the exegesis of the machinery of the inquiry. The inquiry itself, stubbornly ambiguous, is subject only to educated guesses. Like any mystic, Riobaldo finds that a spiritual quest requires the creation of an appropriate vehicle for discovery—a language. His rational process, rather than that of a teller of tales, is to discover for himself the truth of things, to give them a name.[18]

The linguistic artifice is, however, part of the creation of an essentially literary effect, and while both philosophical and religious suggestion abound, the text is designed to convey meaning, to apprehend and transmit signs. Rather than a literary glossolalia, intelligible only to the speaker and his maker, the language of *GSV* is not yet gobbledygook, even though it may strain the reader's sense of an order based on a consistent set of linguistic norms. A native speaker of Portuguese is in some sense a translator when he reads the book, because he is tempted to recast every sentence into conventional signals even as he responds to the ingenuity of the original language. The translator of the work dealing with any language but Portuguese is constrained to give a translation of a translation, because the text must first be rendered into a standard Portuguese in order to sort out meaning before the transference is feasible. The decorations, those possible, may then be readded. This is not the fault of the translator but the function of the structural possiblities of two different languages. In the case of English, the translator is faced with the task of "translating" from an artificial language which takes full advantage of the inflective character of Portuguese into a language which tends to alter meaning largely through the distribution of words rather than the addition of affixes. "Elegant" diction exists (in varying degrees) in both languages, but the production of original phraseology in English is largely a matter of word choice and order, in Portuguese one of word choice and inflection. Since the diction of *GSV* is at once elegant and rustic, the translator at best reproduces the idiosyncracies of the *sujet*, but only occasionally can he reproduce the full range of unconventional signals used in the expository process. *The Devil to Pay in the Backlands* is an admirably competent betrayal of the original from the title on: it sounds very much like a cowboy story, because although the tone is maintained the

perversity of focus is not. As rendered on a movie screen, a scene of
GSV might simply depict the encampment of a band of *jagunços*.
The same scene in the novel is given to the reader not out of focus
but in alternates and multiples, as if shown in 3-D or even 4-D.
Since glasses are not provided, the reader must himself sort out the
planes and angles, but he is not obligated to reduce things to two
dimensions. Since this is a novel which not only shows and tells
simultaneously but also warps and convolutes in the process, both
the cinematic and translational versions are reductive. They can
show and tell what happens (mostly *fabula*), but they cannot reproduce the strategies of other effects. As an example of the selectivity a
translator must observe, the following passage, chosen at random, is
taken from the English translation of GSV. This selection probably
has neither more nor less "distortion" than any other in the novel.
The first comparison shows this standard English translation
alongside the Portuguese original. The second translation of the
same text is an attempt to render into English something like the
diction a Brazilian would "hear" in reading the passage in Portuguese. Elements in parentheses are not provided in the original
but would probably be supplied by most readers subconsciously.
The item in brackets is an alternative translation of the previous
word, and four particularly difficult forms are marked with asterisks.
As a guide for determining the existence or modification of words,
the most popular one-volume Brazilian dictionary has been used.[19]
Naturally some of these words and phrases may exist, but in all
likelihood forms not registered in this standard dictionary are either
neologisms or items of extremely restricted modern usage:

| | |
|---|---|
| Bunches of men, wandering about aimlessly, loafing, or standing around in detachments; some sleeping in the shade like a steer; others stretched out on the ground but not sleeping— just lying there. They were dressed every which way: one fellow wore a wide sash of red wool around his waist; another sported a beaver hat and a black vest of fine cloth, a regular dude; others had on straw rain capes, even though it wasn't raining; | A ajunta, ali, assim, de tantos atrás do ar, na vagagem: manga de homens, por zanzar ou estar à-tôa ou parar formando rodas; ou uns dormindo, como boi malha; ou deitados no chão sem dormir— só aboboravam. Assaz tôda espécie de roupa, divulguei: até sujeito com cinta larga de lã vermelha; outro com chapéu de lebre e colete prêto de fino pano, cidadão; outros com coroça e bedém, mesmo sem chuva nenhuma; |

however, nobody wore anything white, for light-colored clothing makes you an easy target. But never did any of them go about naked or indecently exposed in front of others, that never. Walking or sitting around, playing games, wrestling, chewing strong tobacco and spitting far, or smoking, crumbling tobacco or shredding it in the palm, leisurely—aside from this, all they did was talk. Sometimes they would swap their trifling possessions, things they no longer wanted, bought cheap. But nobody stole! To steal was to risk death! They sang ditties, and some sang herding songs, without cattle. Or looked after their bellies. (*DPB*, pp. 137–38)

só que de branco vestido não se tinha: que com terno claro não se guerreia. Mas jamais ninguém ficasse nú-de-Deus ou indecente composto, no meio dos outros, isso não e não. Andando que sentados, jogando jogos, ferrando queda de braço, assoando o nariz, mascando fumo forte e cuspindo longe, e pitando, picando ou dedilhando fumo no côvo da mão, com muita demora; o mais, sempre no proseio. Aventes, baldrocavam suas pequenas coisas, trem objeto que um tivesse e menos quisesse, que custou barato. E ninguém furtava! Furtasse, era perigar morte. Cantavam cantarol, uns, aboiavam sem bois. Ou cuidavam do espírito da barriga. (*GSV*, pp. 126–27)

The reunion, there, thus, of so many behind the air, loafing: (a) detachment of men, (getting ready to) loiter or hang around, or stop forming circles; or some sleeping, like a spot(ted) steėr; or lying on the ground without sleeping— they just ripened. Tolerably every kind of clothing, I divulged: even a guy with a wide sash of red wool; another with a hare hat and a black vest of fine cloth, (a) citizen; others with straw rain capes and rain tunics, even with no rain whatsoever; only that there were none in white clothing: because one doesn't make war in a light-clolored suit. But nobody ever (should) remain naked as God (made them) or immodestly indecent in the midst of others, that no and no. Walking (as if) sitting, playing games, arm wrestling, blowing their noses, chewing strong tobacco and spitting far, and smoking,

A ajunta, ali, assim, de tantos atrás do ar, na vagagem: manga de homens, por zanzar ou estar á-tôa ou parar formando rodas; ou uns dormindo, como boi malha; ou deitados no chão sem dormir— só aboboravam. Assaz tôda espécie de roupa, divulguei: até sujeito com cinta larga de lã vermelha; outro com chapéu de lebre e colete prêto de fino pano, cidadão; outros com coroça e bedém, mesmo sem chuva nenhuma; só que de branco vestido não se tinha: que com terno claro não se guerreia. Mas jamais ninguém ficasse nú-de-Deus ou indecente composto, no meio dos outros, isso não e não. Andando que sentados, jogando jogos, ferrando queda de braço, assoando o nariz, mascando fumo forte e cuspindo longe, e pitando, picando ou dedilhando fumo no côvo da mão, com muita demora; o

shredding or fingering* tobacco
in the concave of the hand, leisurely;
aside from that, always in chatter.*
Betimes* they would cheat [defraud]
their small things, thing objects
they had and wanted less, bought cheap.
And nobody stole! Were (someone) to
steal was to risk death! They sang
hums,* some, and sang herding songs,
without cattle. Or took care of the
spirit of the belly.

mais, sempre no proseio.
Aventes, baldrocavam suas
pequenas coisas, trem objeto
que um tivesse e menos quisesse, que
custou barato. E ninguém furtava!
Furtasse, era perigar morte. Cantavam
cantarol, uns, aboiavam
sem bois. Ou cuidavam do
espírito da barriga. (GSV, pp. 126–27)

| | |
|---|---|
| *fingering | *dedilhando*, normally used only for the fingering of a musical instrument. |
| *in chatter | *no proseio*, "in the," plus noun invented from the verb *prosear*, "to chat." |
| *Betimes | *Aventes*. Not registered, but possibly derived from the verb *aventar*, "to winnow; to manifest; to discover." |
| *sang hums | *Cantavam cantarol*. *Cantarol* is a neologism apparently based on *cantarola*, "singsong," or *cantarolar*, "to hum." |

Any text translated from Portuguese to English poses some selective problems for the translator. The discussion of this problem has even become a sign of intellectual delinquency in regard to works of art, but this text would appear to deserve some such attention. A truly literal version of anything would come out bizarre in English, but here an attempt has been made to ignore what might be called "standard" stumbling blocks for an intelligible rendition and comment only on those items which probably would provoke a native speaker of Portuguese to stumble, flinch, or wonder. The translator's option in this sort of text is one of degree—how many of the novelties he can or should attempt to include, since the reader may take a deformation as a clumsy translation rather than a faithful one. Notable in this passage is the elliptical quality of the narration. Very often even words not commented here are only understood to be there. This is especially true of verbs, which when they do appear are often in the subjunctive mode without the necessary grammatical support. The conveyance of particular meanings through metaphor ("shade" conveyed by the spots on an animal's hide, "ripening" for inactivity, the "spirit of the belly" for hunger), reduplication ("thing object" is *trem objeto*, both of which mean "thing," though the former is slang, the latter erudite), and neologism (*proseio* and *cantarol*) are also among the easily identifiable characteristics of the prose. Other items in this same passage might well have given the translators cause to write to Guimarães Rosa for clarification, a type of correspondence which itself constitutes one of the more promising types of source material on his work and which is only now coming into print. How a native speaker might react to the original Portuguese of this paragraph is beyond knowing, but certainly many are tempted to read the book with the aid of the dictionary. Even those who feel that their responses are properly attuned may use a dictionary merely to find out whether the vocabulary is invented or only obscure.

This same process of naming, the mystical search for the word, old or new, which can be used to encompass an imponderable phenomenon, has an interesting analog in one of the thematic foci of the novel. The narrative is counterpointed by two motifs, each occurring numerous times throughout the novel. The first is one to which Riobaldo frequently has recourse when the narration becomes too entangled for him to extract precise sequences, or when some incident demonstrates the unexpected nature of the universe: "Living is a dangerous business." The second, though it serves as the book's epigraph, occurs with much less frequency, and (in the original) always in italics, as if it were not really part of Riobaldo's speech at all but an obsessive refrain of extrareal origin: *"The devil in the street, in the middle of the whirlwind."* The devil (and the attributes of his domain—sin, damnation, occult power) occupies a position of extraordinary importance in this work. Again, the process is one of naming; again, the translator is thwarted. By page 33 of the original, Riobaldo has used no less than forty-four different names for the devil, twenty-five of them on a single page. The rendition into English is complicated by the fact that the devil is linguistically more circumscribed in English than in Portuguese: it may be that, whatever the reasons, the concept never gained the status it has in Portuguese as a category of thought.[20] Guimarães Rosa takes advantage of the euphemistic penchant in his language and coins a number of synonyms of his own, the most interesting and effective of which is *O* (literally, "the"), which Pedro Xisto views as not only a letter, a zero, but the final circle in Dante's hell, the irreducible symbolic terminus.[21] The opening pages of *GSV* abound both with names for the devil and with anecdotes about his existence and powers. Riobaldo recounts several tales of possession by the devil and pacts with the devil, speculating on the truth of all this through one of his own earthy conundrums: "Does the devil exist, or doesn't he? That's what I'd like to know. I give up. Look: there is such a thing as a waterfall, isn't there? Yes, but a waterfall is only a high bank with water tumbling over the edge. Take away the water, or level the bank—what becomes of the waterfall? Living is a very dangerous business . . ." (6). José Carlos Garbuglio comments on the rational process involved in this conceit. The two elements that make up the waterfall, the water and the bank, are concrete elements, which, together, make up the third concrete element, the waterfall itself. One supports the other, but the object exists only by composition, which involves not only the concept of singularity and plurality but also that of appearance and reality. The inquiry becomes a dead-end street, because it oversteps the boundaries of logic.[22]

Riobaldo frequently indulges in such digressions, and many of the asides are concerned with the same questions: does the devil exist, and if he does, can mortals enter into pacts with him? The motive force behind this obsessive inquiry is, of course, the ambiguity surrounding Riobaldo's own possible pact with the devil, which might have been the reason things turned out as they did. Riobaldo subscribes to a very un-Roman catholicity of faith, for although he confesses his need for religion and his belief in the efficacy of prayer, he finds the world so crazy that he subscribes to all religions: "Lots of religion, young man. As for me, I never miss a chance. I take advantage of all of them. I drink water from any river" (10). For him, the risks of living are so great that prudence demands an open mind about religion. He prays in the Catholic manner, imitates his friend Quelemém in his spiritist faith (Quelemém is a follower of Alan Kardek), admires and participates in Methodist hymn-singing with another friend. It is thus useless to assume that he believes in the devil merely because he should have a folk Catholic view of the universe. But his obsession is a matter of protesting too much, because he continually asserts his belief in God and hopes to deny the existence of the devil. His inquiry is similar to his own metaphor: What happens to the waterfall (the world) if one of the two elements which make it what it is (good and evil, God and the devil) is absent? The question is never resolved because it cannot be answered, but it continues to haunt him, much like the unanswerable questions posed by Oriental philosophies or even the Western version about whether a tree falling in a deserted forest still makes a noise. Brazilian critics have expended a lot of energy and paper in the process of attempting to ascertain whether or not there really was a pact. The answer is not really provided in the text, because the crux of the mystery is the question about the pact with a devil, real or imagined, and his obsession with the *absence* of the devil.[23] Whether or not there is a devil and there was a pact, the possibilities are a central part of tension and narrative development. In addition, *GSV* is structurally perhaps the most symmetrical of Guimarães Rosa's works. Although the narration is apparently a chaotic, disordered monologue, the novel has the same taut structure as the tales in *Corpo de Baile;* again, the world and the narrative are composed of pairs of opposites. The naive comparative conceit that good cannot exist without evil, or hot without cold, is transformed into a more sophisticated and less secure set of rules, in which certainty is replaced by doubt.

Like a baroque poem, *GSV's* structure is bilaterally symmetrical, and it has a lot in common with an even older tradition: the epic. Some writers have gone to great lengths to determine from just which epic tradition *GSV* derives, and some have even attempted to show that it is not an epic at all. But the narrative shares so many features with different sorts of epic literature that the reader can hardly help making some of the connections, even though he may not be able to identify which particular tradition certain features are based on. With qualifications, Brazilian critics have seen in *GSV* the impact of Greek epic literature, the romance of chivalry, the *chanson de geste,* courtly literature, and the quest of the Holy Grail, to name only the most frequently cited. It is here that the comparison with Tolkien is particularly relevant, because appeal to the reader's sensibilities is made through the same channels that make rewritings of the Arthurian cycle viable literary practice in this century. Whether or not the reader has any scholarly knowledge of epic types is irrelevant—it is not even necessary that he have a very precise memory of it. But it is probably fair to assume that he must at some time have been exposed to epic tradition, or a good deal of the effect will be produced in isolation rather than with the parallel response that remembrance and identification bring.

Two Brazilian critics who have studied this aspect of *GSV* in some detail are Antônio Cândido and M. Cavalcanti Proença. Among the features they enumerate which place the novel in the tradition of epic conventions are the following: the intercalation of convergent narrative episodes, the use of elements taken from real romances (the tale of the leper in the tree), the medieval character of the chieftains (Cavalcanti Proença compares Medeiro Vaz to Charlemagne, Joca Ramiro to St. George), Diadorim's disguise and vow of chastity, the technique of enumerating warriors and their attributes before battle, the treatment of the role of the devil in the climax, the development of characters (Riobaldo, like Roland and Tristan, is illegitimate and gains stature through proof of arms), the importance of rites of initiation and passage, the medieval character of the pact itself (taken, according to Cândido, from the Trial of the Perilous Chapel of the Grail cycle), the passage of the paladin Riobaldo from unknown to chieftain with the appropriate changes of name, and the acquisition of the enchanted steed (Siruiz) by the hero before the final trial.[24] Virtually dozens of other features have been enumerated by other writers, including the tendency to describe *jagunços* physically as knights and the moralizing tone of the entire narrative.[25]

Most writers on this subject have qualified their comments—no one appears to be predicating a literal resurrection of the romance of chivalry or the Homeric poem. One of the clearest distinguishing features, as Cândido notes, is the relative ambiguity of the moral question in *GSV*. In the chivalric tradition and most early epic prose, pillage and plunder were rendered ethically neutral because the larger moral issues were clear. Here, some acts of violence are gratuitous, because the *jagunços* are in effect mercenaries, acting under orders. In addition, although Hermógenes emerges early as an unquestionably evil character and is, in fact, identified by his name and by Riobaldo's assessments as an agent of Satan, numerous questions raised in the narrative fail to find clear resolution, because so much of the work is propped up by speculations on the difference between reality and illusion. However precise the parallels are, there is no question that many effects depend on reader resonance to Riobaldo's position as a singer of heroic deeds and the general quality of the preterite narrative as having taken place in a mythic or legendary space. The book will undoubtedly continue to provide a fertile ground for myth critics of all persuasions, because like both Tolkien and Pynchon, Guimarães Rosa articulates character, episode, time, and even language in a manner undeniably intended to provoke reader consideration or reconsideration of the epic and mythic traditions of his culture.[26]

Aside from the general configuration and narrative idiosyncracy of the tale, there are myriad minor features, some of which appear to be totally out of place, which may prompt yet another reader identification. It is unimportant to belabor authorial intentions in such cases, for some features inevitably do have recognition functions for some readers. In a tale which takes place in central Brazil, parts of it in a desert, it is odd to hear a narrator who presumably has never even seen the ocean remark, "I understood what it meant to be a jagunço, even though I was a sailor on my maiden voyage" (p. 143). Also, the key word *travessia,* which means both "passage" and "crossing," is the last word in the book and only one of numerous words that suggest voyaging. Riobaldo's apparently incongruous penchant for nautical metaphor and seagoing terminology is likely to cause the reader to make a momentary, perhaps subliminal, comparison with the prototypical voyager, Ulysses.[27] Other features reminiscent of early epic literature are Riobaldo's character attributes (though there is some ambiguity about this matter too, Riobaldo would appear to possess the epic heroic virtues of courage and the wisdom of experience), particularly his physical prowess. In the epic tradition, a specific heroic trait was proficiency with a particular weapon; in Riobaldo's case, the rifle. Early heroes were also expected to have a way with words, a talent which Riobaldo demonstrates at every turn. His rambling and highly inventive narrative—the book itself—is the ultimate proof, but he also gained the early admiration of his companions by his eloquence (and courage).[28]

More important than the minutiae, however, is the larger construct involving the dual nature of the fictional universe of *GSV*. The pairing of elements is a feature which both copies and expands upon the conventions of epic literature. In terms of myth, the crucial part of the coupling system is the division of the world into two discrete varieties of space, the boundary marked by the São Francisco River. Antônio Cândido has written a trenchant analysis of this larger dimension of a cosmos of twos, contrasting the home territory of the *jagunços,* a relatively reasonable and ordered place, with that found on the other side of the river, a "kind of legendary space, without geographical boundaries, without precise names, peopled by a

strange race which seems to have emerged from the depths of
time." It is in this "Waste Land" that the equivocal scene of
Riobaldo's pact takes place.[29] The physical nature of this place, the
line that divides it from the rest of the world, the passage necessary
to reach it, are all modeled on the assorted hells and forbidden lands
found in the long tradition of epic literature (in Tolkien, Frodo
Baggins and Sam crossing the desert of Mordor to Mount Doom; in
Pynchon, Slothrop in "The Zone"; and all the earlier trials of heroes
in the damned places which are so often episodes in quests). If this
scene and indeed the rest of the book end up being no more than
imperfect renditions of epic conventions, they are no less impressed
upon the reader as one of the salient features of the story and one of
the few clear approaches to understanding in a book which seems to
deny understanding to many.

An exhaustive study of the epic and mythic qualities of *GSV* will
probably never be made, but it is an area of legitimate concern,
even in so minor an aspect as the names of characters. It should be
recalled that the tradition of naming as a clue to character is not only
a very old one but also one in which the name at first glance may not
mean much.[30] It is thus not only possible but imperative to consider
the business of naming in this book, since all the major characters
and many of the minor ones are designated by symbolic or highly
significant appellations. A name like Riobaldo, hardly a commonplace given name in Portuguese, may jar the reader's sense of
appropriateness as much as any of the invented words in the text,
unless consideration of its symbolic potential is made. Riobaldo is
usually analyzed as an agglutination of *rio*, "river," and *baldo*, "(in)
vain," since the narrator is identified repeatedly in the text with the
Urucúia River, a "vain" watercourse because it does not flow into
the sea but rather "disappears"—into the São Francisco.[31] Another
possibility, which the critics have not suggested, is that *baldo* may
be used, as it was in Jorge Amado's *Jubiabá*, as a shortened form of
*balduíno*, a corruption of the name of the Baldwin locomotive and a
word still used in the folk speech of Brazil as a synonym for "powerful (machine)."[32] Like many of the characters in the novel, Riobaldo
also has alternate names: *Tatarana* (from *taturana* or *lagarta-de-
fogo*, literally, "fire caterpillar," so designated because of his skill
with firearms) and *Urutu Branco* ("white rattlesnake"). These names
appear to coincide with his development as a leader, just as epic
heroes "earned" or revealed secret names. Riobaldo is one of the

most complex characters in the book, largely because the rhetorical design allows him the latitude to play his own somewhat theatrical self as well as to inform and shape his other self, the character in the past narration. In one guise or another, Riobaldo plays the parts of narrator and character, leader and follower, victim and victor, innocent and omniscient, bandit and lover. In some senses, he is also the hero, the (possible) pactmaker, the mystic. Since all these characteristics are presented contrapuntally and in largely unpredictable order, he is to the reader an elusive but fascinating character, constantly vacillating between truth and lies, love and hate. It may not be possible to select from all these attributes the most important ones, but the dialectics that principally inform the plot and produce the major tensions are the quest for an impossible love and the problematical nature of a compact with Satan. A bandit and killer, a *macho*, he loves another man. Also ingenuous and superstitious, he is haunted by the dialectic of good and evil. How can he love a man and remain a man himself? How can he deny the devil without denying God?

Though Diadorim is rhetorically distanced from the reader, she is in many senses Riobaldo's creation, since all that can be known of her is the narrator's version, and she is thus no less dialectical than her explainer. In addition, although clues to her true gender are scattered throughout the text, outright statement of this fact is withheld until the last part of the narrative, and she thus functions as a (disguised) male through most of the story. As a character, Diadorim is an androgynous being, both man and woman, both divine and diabolical: negative, dark, and feminine (Yin); positive, bright, and masculine (Yang). The suggestive possibilities of her name have been examined by a number of writers, and, like Riobaldo, she uses different names as her role fluctuates. The masculine name she uses with the group is Reinaldo, suggesting counseling and governing functions,[33] the name known only to Riobaldo is Diadorim, and her real name is Maria Deodorina da Fé Bettancourt Marins ("Mary" and "Faith" being the two most suggestive components). Each of these names is amenable to etymological examination, but the most important one is the one most often used by the narrator, Diadorim. Numerous possibilities have been suggested for the figurative meanings of this name, some of them obscure enough to satisfy the most demanding adepts of the arcana of names: *dia* + *doron*, "through" + "gift"; *di* + *adorar*, "two + "to adore," or "the doubly adored"; *diá* + *dor* + *in*, "intermediary of pain."[34] The components most likely to provoke a native speaker of Portuguese to react, however, would be *dia*, "day," *dor*, "pain, suffering," *dó*, "pity, compassion," and *ador*, from *adorar*, "to adore." Antônio Cândido suggests that the name can be viewed by analogical link to the Portuguese name for Theodore, *Deodoro*, which derives from *Teodoro*. Applying this analogy with the alteration of a single phoneme, the result is *Diadoro—Tiadoro*, "I love you"[35] (the final *-im* is diminutive). The other important allusion contained in the name is *diá*, one of the many names in Portuguese for the devil. The hypothesis is made more plausible by the fact that *diá* is one of the names Riobaldo actually uses in reference to Satan. Because of its phonetic structure, Diadorim's name has a larger suggestive range than that of Riobaldo, but it is reasonable to assume that at least some of these possibilities are intended. Since Diadorim is at the center of Riobaldo's two preoccupations, love and the devil, the credible intimations would appear to be *diá*, "devil," and *Diadoro—Tiadoro*, "I love you." To carry the etymological game to a suitably recondite length, it might be noted that the probable functional prototype for Diadorim is Hermaphroditus, son of Hermes and Aphrodite, who was blessed with the beauty of both parents. Whatever indications may be implied from Diadorim's name, her/his role in the tale is at least as complex as Riobaldo's. Like him, Diadorim is presented as a dialectical personage, embodying at once the characteristics of warrior and sweetheart, courage and tenderness. She is also involved in the dialectic involving reality and illusion, and she is the central all-encompassing figure in the metaphysical stratum of *GSV*.

One other character in the novel of sufficient importance to merit this kind of etymological study is Hermógenes, the pactmaker with the devil and representative of evil. One writer has hypothesized that the name was chosen for the suggestive capacity of the Greek root *hermós* to indicate that, like the devil, Hermógenes is a closed thing, hermetic, noting that the villain's rebellion against Joca Ramiro is like that of Lucifer against God, both as a situation and in terms of Hermógenes' behavior.[36] There is no question that Riobaldo intends to link Hermógenes to the dark forces of the universe through all kinds of association, though this particular etymology is quite an obscure one. But Riobaldo does indulge in a lengthy discussion of Hermógenes' pact with the devil, and he claims to have taken an instant dislike to the man from the outset, though he served in the faction under his leadership before the treacherous murder of Joca Ramiro. After the murder, Riobaldo uses the uncapitalized form "hermógenes" both as a plural referent to the villains synonymous with "traitors" and as another of the alternate forms for "devil." The name itself seems to refer to Hermes, suggesting perhaps something like "of Hermes born," and numerous attributes of the ancient deity are easily applicable to the principal villain of the tale. Hermes, like many of the early gods, was a complex and contradictory being, but some of his characteristics coincide perfectly with those of Hermógenes. Aside from his role as patron of thieves, Hermes was known for his craftiness and stealth—he functioned as the sacrificial herald of the gods and the guide for the dead (in Hades). Particularly interesting is the role of Hermes as the god of roads, particular emphasis having been given his activities at crossroads.[37] Hermógenes made his pact with the devil, as the folk belief dictates, at a crossroads, and his role in the action as the consummate thief and master of stealth (he is known to have an uncanny nose for both sides of ambush) derives, it may be assumed, from his commerce with Satan. And his last act, before he presumably makes his final journey to Hades, is as an agent of destiny, announcing and performing the sacrifice of Diadorim. Interestingly, Hermógenes possesses only the redeeming qualities of craft and courage—unlike the other major characters, he has no positive benevolent attributes, no soul.

In Riobaldo's view of things, the only force other than evil deserving of obsessive attention is love. Like evil, love has numerous declensions, and it is presented again in a complex interrelationship with other elements. The most apparent pair-opposition is that between the love that he had for the whore Nhorinhá, a purely sensual love, and that he holds for his sweetheart Otacília, an idealized, chivalric love. There is also a third kind, the unconsummated love for Diadorim, which exists in opposition to each of the others. The temporal relationship of forms of love is also important—his passion for Nhorinhá is preterite and remembered, that for Otacília present (he is married to her), that for Diadorim at best subjunctive, since it became possible only with her death. It might be argued that the simplest opposition would be that between profane love (Nhorinhá) and sacred love (Otacília), but it would seem more appropriate to designate his relationship with Otacília as merely courtly in the past, almost characterless in the present. His love for Diadorim was the only truly spirtual one, and remained so only by the intercession of destiny (or evil), and it thus contains all the elements contained in both the others. Here the dialectical scheme may be said to break down, because of the production of a (final) synthesis. But Diadorim, the androgyne, has during the story demonstrated at least the promise of both the permitted and forbidden kinds of love, and she also contains in her name and being the (devil's) capacity to tempt and not deliver. A being who at first suggests ambivalance, Diadorim is at last the central ambiguous being, the most complete of Guimarães Rosa's frequent enigmatic characters.[38]

In a book with such an abundance of symbolic possibilities, the temptation to read symbolically is naturally strong. Anybody who has ever observed a course in freshman English is aware that the pursuit of symbols seems indeed to be a deeply ingrained natural urge. But it is an urge which needs disciplining, and books like GSV seem to provoke the most outlandish responses in the incautious, merely because symbolic potential appears on so many levels and in so many disparate places. Mary Daniel warns that there is probably not a coherent system of symbols in the book, however, or, if one exists, it is probably not an intentional one.[39] Consciously or not, Guimarães Rosa nevertheless exploits with some consistency a pattern which forces recognition of the probably representational functions of certain referents. Some of these are taken from the traditions of European and Brazilian folklore (the owl as the messenger of destiny, the white horse of the paladin), others from Guimarães Rosa's own symbolic catalog (as in *Corpo de Baile*, the *buriti* palm has broad symbolic potential), still others from fortuitous linguistic or metaphorical connections. In the last category, the importance of the word *sertão* not only as a geographical limit but as affective space should be noted. During the heat of the final climactic battle, Riobaldo is forcing himself to be brave when he thinks he hears someone (perhaps himself) laughing: "I refused to think about what I didn't want to think it was, and assured myself it was a false notion. I was about to let out a curse: 'Satan! Filthy One! ' but I said only: 'S—Sertão—Sertão—' " (479). The Portuguese word he uses here for "Satan" is phonetically only a hair's breadth from the word *sertão*, and thus the devil and the place are fused by a linguistic accident. This may suggest that the *sertão* is hell or it may merely indicate Riobaldo's irrationality. But is certainly makes possible a symbolic linkage between two concepts which have similarities only on a phonetic level. The danger is that the reader's symbolic antennae may become oversensitized, that he will attempt to enforce unilateral patterns on symbols which are intended to be ambiguous. The element which has attracted the most such attention is the central personage, Diadorim-Reinaldo-Maria Deodorina, probably because everything from the Virgin Mary to God Him/Herself is suggested by one or another of the facets of this character.

The usual expectation of a critical review is that it tell the reader of the book something he may not have known and advise the potential reader whether or not he should read the book. These are legitimate demands, and at the very least readers might require the critic to tell them what he thinks the book is. Is it a novel? If so, what kind—an adventure tale, an epic, a love story? A novel of ideas? A morality tale? Or is it a romance? An allegory? What is it like—is it modern or old-fashioned, funny or serious? Is it interesting? Is it really worth all the trouble? The answer to all these questions in the case of *GSV* is yes. It is also a long list of other things, which somewhat complicates the selective process ordinarily used in finding adequate descriptive terminology. The reading of *GSV* is in some ways a quest in itself, because the reader is constantly attempting to find a fixed point at which he can feel certain about things. But, as José Carlos Garbuglio writes, that point never appears, and the probabilities open in a fan. Every reading of the book is different from the first one, and from all others, so Garbuglio suggests what he calls an "ultrareading,"[40] a sort of agglutinate that might embrace elements from all the possible ways of reading the work into one mind-boggling synthesis. It might be advanced that such a reading, if it existed, would pose a danger to the affective circuitry of the ultrareader—it is thus perhaps fortunate that it is impossible.

Proof that other readings are possible abounds in the bibliography on *GSV*. One of them, easily incorporable into the ultrareading, is that of Dante Moreira Leite, appended here for the sake of illustration. Leite's reading, which is a provocative one, insists that *GSV* be read as a psychoanalytic session, in which the patient (Riobaldo) is talking to the psychoanalyst (the interlocutor, and, by extension, the reader). The confessional nature of first-person narration is naturally one of the justifications for this approach, but as Leite notes, a good deal of this narrative consists of the speaker's attempts to clear up the muddy waters of his past, largely by free association. It is also noted that Riobaldo mentions early in the narrative (and only once by name) one of his mother's "protectors," a man named Gramacêdo, whose memory inspires in Riobaldo considerable emotion, mostly hate. The patient then veers off to recount the tale of the *jagunços*, in which the matter of dominance of one group over another and one man over others is discussed. A series of father figures (the *jagunço* chieftains) is related, culminating in the patient's single mention of his "father's house," which is accompanied by a feeling of power. At last, the patient accepts the ultimate available father figure—the devil. The ambiguity at first demonstrated becomes a kind of psychiatric ambivalence, and at last, Leite asserts in some rather convoluted logic, Riobaldo can be viewed as being troubled because he committed a sin—that of Oedipus.[41]

It would be unfortunate to limit a reading of GSV to this and nothing more, but this analysis deserves at least to be included as complementary to a structural, mythic, or sociological reading. It has been argued that the Brazilian novel is a particularly deterministic form—that is, that it has historically operated under the influence of one or another of four principal lines of intellection: biological, psychological, sociological, or aestheticist. GSV is a singular example of a novel constructed under the influence of all these deterministic forms,[42] which implies that any view of the book restricted to merely one of these lines of analysis is inherently fragmentary. GSV is one of the best justifications in modern Brazilian fiction for an eclectic criticism, for though numerous critical approaches can provide insight into the workings of the novel, no single one has yet shown itself adequate to a full discussion of the book's multiple effects. And each different view may provide negative as well as positive reactions. An alternate angle may only convince some readers of the book's unreadability, others of its archness. But even the most opprobrious of these readings is apt to reveal something more about the novel's scope of inquiry, though that in itself may not be a particular source of satisfaction to all readers.

Clearly some approaches are more useful than others, however: the hazard would appear to be not simply the adoption of one method but the issuance of terminal judgments based on a single view. Because the novel is on so many levels constructed along the lines of a dialectic, some consideration of the doubling phenomenon is indispensable. Because it patently reproduces or revises epic and mythic traditions, these must be considered. Because it is written in a nonexistent, perverse, insinuative language, some kind of linguistic analysis is required. Because of the complexity and importance of point of view, time, and their attendant entanglements, the rhetorical design begs attention. Because of the importance of conceptual abstracts, especially moral ones, an ethical or even ecclesiastical reading is useful. And because of the diversity of psychological and symbolic innuendo, some consideration must be made of the figurative or representational patterns of the work. It would even be fruitful to examine the fascinating interplay between the two inclusive sources, the popular and the erudite, which are not only the most general first step in the dialectic scheme but also encompass most of the other elements, since such features as language, motifs, and philosophical conceits are probably all traceable to either a folk origin or a learned root.[43]

One engrossing example of a doublet on these lines is the motif of the girl disguised as a man. The literarily sophisticated reader will no doubt recall the mythical importance of the hermaphrodite and the importance of this particular kind of duplicity in a number of other literary traditions, notably those of the Renaissance and Middle Ages. The hypothetical illiterate listener (and, if he is Brazilian, probably the sophisticate) would likely recognize the same motif from a different source. Though the ultimate origin of the two versions is probably a single tale, a folk rendition of the story is well known, notably in *literatura de cordel,* the only printed form of Brazilian folk literature. This literature, derived from the old troubador tradition, still thrives in Brazil's interior. An example of this particular motif is the folk poem "O Vaqueiro que Virou Mulher e Deu à Luz" ("The Cowboy Who Turned Into a Woman and Gave Birth"),[44] one strophe of which reads:

> Nobody knows why
> Her sex was hidden,
> By the parents of this innocent,
> Right after birth,
> Although a girl she was
> Dressed as a boy. (5)

Yet another illustrative device might be to study facets of the novel with appropriate parallels in Guimarães Rosa's other works. Franklin de Oliveira notes that several characters and incidents in *GSV* are prefigured in *Corpo de Baile*, including the pact (Miguilim, in "Campo Geral"), the hidden sex of Diadorim (Dom Varão, from Joana Xaviel's intercalated tale in "Uma Estória de Amor"), Otacília (who appears in "Lélio e Lina"), and numerous others.[45] Another inside source might be the composition essays appearing in *Tutaméia*, which reveal something about Guimarães Rosa's sources and his attitudes about fictional constructs.

None of this is intended to suggest that the book is impossibly complex, nor necessarily wider ranging than books in other languages. But it is meant to convey a sense of the book's continuing impact in Brazil and some idea about its possible literary relatives in other countries. Like any work of fiction, *GSV* establishes its own limits and works within a finite code of signals and potentialities. But because it is an open work and a very pithy one, it is not too much to surmise that it will remain one of those rare volumes like *Don Quixote* upon which no one will ever have the satisfaction of offering the last word.

CHAPTER 4

# Primeiras Estórias:
## *At the Threshold*

*P* *rimeiras Estórias (First Stories)*, a book containing twenty-one short narratives, was published in 1962. It appeared in English in 1968 under the title *The Third Bank of the River and Other Stories*, in a fine translation by Barbara Shelby.[1] It is claimed that Guimarães Rosa chose both the format and the title of his new book after a turning point in his own life, a near-fatal heart attack which he suffered in 1958.[2] These are the "first stories" following whatever revelations might have accrued from the crisis, and they bespeak an author radically changed in outlook. Had his critics and faithful readers attempted to predict a fourth book, logic would probably have led them to anticipate something vaster and more ambitious than *Grande Sertão*, though prudence and an awareness of Guimarães Rosa's genteel intransigence might have produced more outlandish predictions, or, in the cautious, no predictions at all. Perhaps Guimarães Rosa considered the possibility of ever-progressive inclusion and thought it a bad idea. Perhaps the illness itself changed his mind. But these *estórias* (a term for "story" the author rescued from disuse to avoid the ambiguity of the homophone *história*, which means both "story" and "history") are certainly his first.

Some of the characteristics of the early Guimarães Rosa are still present in the book: there persists a fascination with the word and its potential, a view of the world sharpened by a sense of irony, and an engrossment with the duplicity of occurrences. But the focus here is microscopic rather than cosmic, and the narrative process relies less on carefully paced climax than on epiphany. The controlled turbulence of the earlier diction has also been replaced by an incisive, condensed vocabulary and syntax which is something beyond mere economy of expression.

An element common to all the first stories is a modification of a substratum found in the previous three books. In *Sagarana*, the

89

plots were all more or less conventionally constructed around the movement of protagonists toward some desired end, which is one reason that resonance in that work carries such a heavy charge of patterned familiarity, since the patterns were largely derived from traditional narrative forms. In *Corpo de Baile*, most plots were constructed around tensions, which implies tension relief as a principal goal of the characters and a principal source of reader experience. And in *Grande Sertão*, both the action and the mystical stratum were connected to yet another traditional narrative device, the quest motif. The stories in *PE* are also constructed around the hermeneutics of becoming, but here the anxiety and tension are relatively reduced in importance—not merely because each tale must come to a climax in a short time due to the brevity of the narrative, but because discovery and fruition are here as much part of effect as the search itself, previously so important. The point in a tale identifiable as a climax in the first three works has been seen as a point at which separate narrative planes finally coincided or crossed, where dramatic situations were unraveled, where mysteries or secrets were revealed, or where obscure motivations were clarified. Even in cases of highly ambiguous characters, such as Dona Rosalina, in "Lélio e Lina," the denouement provided the reader with a satisfactory number of speculative possibilities about motivations and a plot closure which indicated completion and unrepeatableness. But in *PE* the discoveries made are of such an unorthodox nature, and the characters making the discoveries of such unfamiliar configuration, that released tension is at best oblique and understated; often it is subliminal. Another feature which works on behalf of attenuated response is the highly elliptical diction. As in all of Guimarães Rosa's works, language in *PE* is itself both attractive for its originality and somewhat unsettling because of its unconventionality. Like the structures of the tales themselves, however, language in these stories reverses the visible trend toward gigantism and shrinks to a laconic, eloquent shorthand. Where before Guimarães Rosa could pause and indulge in a leisurely display of linguistic symphonics, the stories in *PE* are delivered in minor keys, in eighth notes, and the loss of a single phrase is disproportionate to its length.

Plot summaries, which have deservedly fallen into general disrepute, have been shown to be of even less than the usual utility in the case of Guimarães Rosa's works. In this book, plot itself is both less revealing and less subject to summary than in the earlier volumes. But the stories in *PE* all share certain characteristics which facilitate useful generalizations. Most critics have commented on the frequent presence in these narratives of deranged or socially marginal characters, for example. One writer has advanced the idea that eccentric acts and "magic helpers" are of key importance, along with children, as determiners of narrative form in *PE*.[3] The feature itself is not precisely a new one for Guimarães Rosa, but only in *Corpo de Baile* were madmen and children of pivotal importance, and then in only half the stories. Here, there is a being of special sensibility and vaguely alien nature as a principal in every tale. Most readers will probably leave the book with an awareness that some pretty peculiar characters are at the center of the transformations operated in *PE*, but it may be less apparent that they share certain traits. At least two of the types included here, children and bullies, may not strike all readers as at all eccentric, but it is fair to say that an appreciation for the implied oddness of these personages is in itself an important first step in grasping the processes at work in the book. It may seem artificial to attempt to establish a relationship between a story whose principal character is a wonder-struck little boy on his first plane ride and another featuring a slovenly Italian immigrant who lives in a haunted house and eats lettuce by the bucketful, but both these stories derive effects from reader appreciation of the roles of characters disengaged from certain aspects of social machinery. The perceptions of and about such beings comprise the meat of the stories.

The feature which all these beings share is their status, temporary or permanent, as outsiders or marginals. Since they are in but not of the locality of the tale, they enjoy both the relative safety of distance and the burden of increased perceptions, something in the manner of a de Tocqueville, whose Frenchness allowed him to observe another society as both grander and more outlandish than any insider could have found it. The example is overly simple, because the vantage points in *PE* are neither political nor quite so systematic, since in at least one case ("The Mirror") the alien being is the subject of his own observation, but the outsider's position is nevertheless metaphorically comparable. In addition to the quality of strangeness or not-belonging, every tale in the book involves a transformation or a becoming—a realization that something important has happened or is about to happen. Since these same marginals are always either responsible for the transformation or the only ones to perceive it, a useful term, applicable to the entire range of eccentrics, might be derived from the anthropological concept of "liminality," or the quality of being "at the threshold."[4] As in "O Recado do Morro" *(Corpo de Baile)*, children operate on the threshold along with the mad and the inspired, and as in "Conversation Among Oxen" *(Sagarana)*, animals have the same capability as nonparticipant, prescient creatures. In four of the tales of *PE* a child or a group of children functions as the prismatic expanding device of the perception; in one, the liminal being is a cow. The latter example (from "Cause and Effect") is the only isolated liminal animal in the book and the only creature that functions as a "magic helper" in the traditional, folkloric sense. In another three stories, liminality is provided by hoodlums, either in fact or because of a sort of reciprocal perception, in which their very status as tough guys separates them from the other characters. In the twelve remaining tales, liminal beings are of much more obviously alien nature. In these stories, the liminal characters are either inexplicably eccentric, mentally deficient, or outright mad.

These liminal beings either precipitate or perceive the basic transformation, but each transformation in turn depends on an agent or vehicle. As each threshold is approached, an object in the tale assumes particular importance. The process here is similar to the traditional short story use of "active detail," in which one item in the tale becomes a key element in the climax and denouement, usually by repetition. The vehicles in the stories of *PE* range from the very traditional, such as the message-bearer in "Honeymoons," to the scarcely believable, such as the piece of cow dung in "The Aldacious Navigator."

The final common element is the transformation itself, which may be simply a revelation of an unknown truth, in the mold of the traditional short story, or a transcendence, in which the events and characters of the story culminate in an unexpectedly complete resolution. This final becoming, the transformation, is frequently of such an abstract or mysterious nature that any attempt to reduce it to a word or phrase is bound to be thwarted. Transformation is, in fact, the single most important source of effect in the stories of *PE*, but in no story is the change simply one of category or status. The changes which operate in *PE* may depend on an awareness of the duplicity of things; on an appreciation for the capacity things have for appearing to assume new attributes, without actually changing;

they may be dependent on the hypersensitivity of the narrator or a liminal being; they may imply second sight. Following the order of the stories in the English version (different from the order in the original), the basic elements of each story are as follows:

"The Thin Edge of Happiness." A boy (liminal) discovers happiness and sadness. Agent: a turkey.

"Tantarum, My Boss." A madman (liminal) transcends age and evil. Vehicle: a wild horse.

"Substance." A man and a mysterious (liminal) girl discover transcendent love. Vehicle: manioc flour.

"Much Ado." A man climbs a palm tree in a public square (liminal act) and becomes a symbol. Vehicle: a palm tree.

"A Woman of Good Works." A murderess (liminal) achieves grace. Vehicle: a dead dog.

"The Aldacious Navigator." Some children (one especially liminal) achieve wonder and learn about love. Vehicle: a lump of cow dung.

"Honeymoons." A man rediscovers love and courage. Vehicle: a messenger.

"A Young Man, Gleaming, White." A population discovers *saudade*[5] and the proximity of death. Vehicle: a young man from space.

"The Horse That Drank Beer." A crazy (liminal) Italian reveals the secrets of a house and the beauty behind ugliness. Vehicle: a beer-drinking horse.

"Nothingness and the Human Condition." A man gives away all his possessions (liminal act) and transcends himself. Vehicle: a ranch house.

"The Mirror." A man loses and rediscovers himself (liminal state). Vehicle: a mirror.

"Cause and Effect." A man finds love. Agent: a cow (liminal).

"My Friend the Fatalist." An eccentric (liminal) shows a man how to free himself from the terrorism of a gunman (also liminal). Vehicle: a gun.

"No Man, No Woman." A boy-man (liminal) reaches understanding and remembrance. Vehicle: a mysterious (liminal) young woman.

"Hocus Psychocus." A group of children (liminal) learn the truth of falsehood, the reality of illusion. Vehicle: a school play.

"The Third Bank of the River." A man demonstrates the potential grace of obstinacy by spending his life in a boat (liminal act). Vehicle: a canoe.

"The Dagobé Brothers." A frightened murderer (liminal) gets a reprieve from death. Vehicles: three (liminal) bullies and a corpse.

"The Girl From Beyond." A mysterious (liminal) little girl learns to perform miracles. Vehicle: a frog.

"Soróco, His Mother, His Daughter." A town learns about separation when two feeble-minded (liminal) inhabitants leave. Vehicle: a song.

"Notorious." A bandit (liminal) and a doctor learn of fame and courage. Vehicle: a word.

"Treetops." A boy (liminal) rediscovers happiness. Agent: a toucan.

These instant resumés are highly reductive, and in some cases the elements chosen as major features are somewhat arbitrarily selected. The feature least subject to clear explanation is the element discovered, learned, achieved, revealed, or transcended. It is most appropriate that the title story of the English version is "The Third Bank of the River," because that third bank—the unexpected dimension of reality—is the real terminus of theme in all the stories. How precisely to explain the third bank is a problem both the critic and the reader face, though most readers will sense it without much difficulty, and those who do not will not be much helped by the best elucidation. This is the feature which most easily likens *PE* to Guimarães Rosa's other works—the reader is pressed not only to suspend disbelief but to indulge in an act of faith. If he cannot discern a river's third bank after reading the book, no amount of discourse will remedy his shortsightedness.

In addition, some of the items designated "vehicles" or "agents" may be merely one of several possible items in the tale. In only three of the stories have I chosen to use the term "agent" rather than "vehicle," because in these three tales the revelation is accomplished in a manner somewhat less passive or accidental than in other stories. It is worth noting that in all these cases the agent is an animal. The most active of these agents is the cow in "Cause and Effect," in which the animal agent, reminiscent of the little dust-brown donkey of *Sagarana*, demonstrates the familiar anthropomorphic intelligence of animals in previous works, as well as the magical quality necessary for reinforcing the man's resolve and bringing about the denouement. Newly purchased, the cow decides to run away and return to its original home, and the man sets out after her almost as a whim. When the cow continues to elude him, his determination becomes an obsession. They reach the end of the quest, and in a very abrupt turn the cow loses all importance as the young man sees the real reason he has been brought to this place: "To a circle of people. To the four young ladies of the house. To one of them, the second oldest. She was tall, fair, and amiable. She disconcealed herself from him. Had they unexpected each other? The youth understood himself." The narrator intervenes directly to provide the denouement: "There is nothing absurd: the honey of enchantment comes at this point in the tale, and the ring of the enchanted. They loved each other. And the cow—hey diddle-diddle, the cow came home" (153).

The other two stories with animal agents are the tales which frame the volume. As in *Corpo de Baile*, the first and last tales in the book feature the same protagonist, though here the little boy of the first tale is still a little boy in the last. In both stories the major event is an airplane flight, and in both the agent of revelation is a bird. The airplane itself might be identified as a sort of auxiliary vehicle in both tales. In "The Thin Edge of Happiness" the wonder of a first airplane ride expands, in the boy's eyes, to a sort of generalized awe at things in the world. Later, when he sees the turkey, it seems to be altogether the most handsome of the many handsome objects in the world. The turkey is killed to provide a festive meal; the boy despairs. But then he discovers another turkey, and he realizes that the object it is furiously pecking at on the ground is the head of the other turkey. In "Treetops," the book's final tale (fortunately re-tained in place in the English version), the same boy flies an airplane to the same city, but this time he is being sent away from home because his mother is gravely ill, perhaps dying. Another agent-object in this story is a little monkey doll which his relatives have given the boy to distract him from his anxiety about his mother. But the real agent of transformation is the toucan he dis-covers in the yard of his uncle's house. During the boy's stay away from home, the bird comes to assume great importance as the one reliable thing of beauty in a world gone awry. When news arrives that the mother has recovered, the boy makes the return trip on the airplane and realizes he has left behind his monkey doll. But the steward on the plane returns to him the doll's hat, which was thrown away on the flight out. The boy starts to cry, but suddenly he is able to recapture for an instant the feeling and presence of all the things important to him—his mother, the doll, the dawn, "—the flight of the toucan, as he came to eat berries in the golden treetop, in the high valleys of the dawn, there close to the house. Only that. Only everything" (238). Both these stories articulate, through a child's simultaneous sense of vulnerability and wonder, the repeatability and elusiveness of rapture, and a sense of its presense in unexpected places and unlikely times.

In four other stories of quite varied effect and dissimilar vehicles, children act as the receptors or transmitters of revelation. In "The Aldacious Navigator," the central liminal character is a little girl whose gifts of perception and expression parallel those of the author. The story takes place one rainy morning on a ranch and ends the same afternoon. The little girl is entertaining herself and the other children with a story about love, which she is attempting to understand. The story is progressively revised throughout the day as the little girl polishes the imagined story and her ideas on the theme. When the rain ends, the children all go out to play, and the little girl discovers a lump of cow dung with a mushroom sprouting forth from it. The cow pie becomes the "aldacious navigator," and when it is finally carried off by the current, now bedecked with flowers and leaves, the story can be finished, love understood. Perceptions in this story are skewed in favor of the marvelous not only because the protagonists are children, but because they are not merely small adults but true threshold beings. Gypsy and Zito are "poised on the edge of reality," and when Imp is pressed for a good denouement for her story within the story, her ending has the novel configuration expected of liminals: "The ocean carried them esthetically along. They went in the ship without being alone, and the ship was nicer and nicer, the ship. . . . That's what it was. And it turned into fireflies" (82, 83).

A story of similar configuration is "The Girl From Beyond," in which the central figure shares Imp's hypersensitivity to her environment, though here the girl performs physical rather than linguistic miracles, and at the end attains something akin to sainthood rather than simply insight. In both cases, the stories imply comprehension of transcendent magnitude, a grasp of the answers to questions beyond the asking in ordinary people. The most abstractive such question is posed in "No Man, No Woman," in which the entire tale takes place in a doubtful, contingent space. The protagonist of the tale is a little boy, who is reliving or attempting to remember events which took place in this enigmatic cosmos. The Child in this story is aggressively liminal, since he is consciously attempting to identify and cross a threshold. Another character, who might be construed as the only character in the book to have crossed the threshold before the tale begins, is Nenha, a woman "most unbelievably old," who resides in the house and is cared for by the old Man, the Maiden, and the Youth. It appears that the old Man, like the other characters, is poised on the edge of some revelation or occurrence rather than beyond. After the Maiden rejects the Youth, the Child rides off with him, returns to the house of his parents, and instantly recognizes himself as changed, alienated from his parents. This tale contains the clearest example of liminality as a true "rite of passage," though the highly ambiguous context makes it impossible to define the precise nature of the state passed.

Another tale featuring liminal children takes place in a boarding school, and the threshold here involves virtually all the characters. The narrator of "Hocus Psychocus" is a boy who acts as prompter for the play the group is about to perform. To prevent the other boarders at the school from finding out what work is being rehearsed, the players invent another story, which they pass off as the plot of the play. On opening night the lead actor is unexpectedly called away, and the narrator, not prepared to perform all the lines as stand-in, falls back on the invented story. The troupe launches into a performance of the nonexistent script, delighting themselves and the audience with their execution. Since the play has never actually been written, however, it has no end, so the prompter ad-libs a climax by falling off the stage.

The fusion of the serious and the comical is common in the narratives of *PE*. In some cases the humorous element derives from tone, and in others it derives from the comic unfolding of events. In four stories, two very serious and two quite funny, the transformation of the tale hinges on the commission of an illogical or bizarre act. These actions, all undertaken on the spur of the moment, are decisive acts which transform the central character and his relationship to those around him. Each action is undertaken after a momentous decision, the motive for which is unexplained. The four decisions: to climb a tree, to spend life in a canoe, to give away wealth, to murder a nephew. "Much Ado," a narrative recounted in what might be called "first-person manic," concerns the surprising appearance one day of a man in a palm tree in a public square. The phenomenon naturally draws a crowd, then police, then firemen. When it is discovered that the man in the tree is not, as suspected, the Secretary of Finance, he disrobes, thus maintaining his importance. When the man finally decides to descend from the palm tree, the crowd becomes hostile, until the man shouts an appropriate slogan and regains heroic stature. In this tale, the liminal act itself functions as a vehicle for revelation, for the presence of the man in the tree, when it has happened, is an ineluctable fact. What concerns the bystanders is that if the man falls from the tree the act will lose impact for lack of an explanation. He does not fall, but the explanation is never provided, at least not by the author.

Another tale which derives from a liminal act by an apparently normal person is the title story of the English version, "The Third Bank of the River." The first-person narrator tells that his father, without explanation, orders a canoe made. When it is finished, he says good-bye and paddles into the middle of the river, where he remains. And there he stays, a living monument to the incongruous, until, years later, the son decides to go tell his father that it is all right, that he will take his father's place in the canoe. At the last moment the son panics and flees. The man disappears, and the son longs for a canoe to die in. The precise significance of the act is never provided, though the title itself suggests the sort of affective spatial dislocation involved in acts of transcendence. A third story based on such an act is "Nothingness and the Human Condition," in which a character called Uncle Man' Antônio, following the death of his wife, divests himself of all his earthly possessions, gives the money to his daughter, and dies. After the funeral, the house containing his body catches fire and burns to the ground. In this case the eccentric act is comparable to ritual death preparations, though there is no indication that the man knew when he would die and no logical justification for his extravagance. Similar is the case of "Tantarum, My Boss," a decidedly liminal character by reason of his impending death and long-standing madness. Tantarum decides one morning to ride off to town to murder his nephew. On the way to town, he manages to assemble an entourage of adventurers and curiosity seekers, who follow the quixotic old man into town. When he arrives at his nephew's house, Tantarum delivers a garbled but apparently moving speech, the final proof of his heroism. All four of these characters arrive at a threshold by adopting apparently antisocial behavior. By crossing the boundaries of propriety they cross the threshold, into a state beyond the boundaries of ordinary experience.

Another character similar to Tantarum, in that he is presented by the narrator as vaguely daft from the outset, is the Italian immigrant in "The Horse That Drank Beer." In both cases eccentricity functions as the main character's principal trait and the characteristic which allows him to obtain something like a state of grace when he crosses the limen. The Italian is a rather less sanitary eccentric, but as his successive secrets (a horse that in fact drinks beer, then a stuffed horse, and finally a horribly disfigured brother) are stripped away, his erratic behavior appears not only less aberrant, but altogether laudable. In both cases recognition that the threshold has been crossed is provided by the narrator, and in both cases the main character at that point moves from absurdity to solemnity.

The least clearly liminal story in the book is "Honeymoons," in which the narrator, a rancher named Joaquim Norberto, is the most eccentric character. Norberto undergoes a manic phase because of the dramatic threshold, which involves the arrival of a message announcing that a young couple is eloping and will spend some time at the ranch. Since it is feared that the girl's relatives will take vengeance, elaborate defense preparations are made. The combination of bellicose logistics and nuptial arrangements puts Joaquim Norberto back into a state of battle preparedness, ready for either the battlefield or the bed, and his diction becomes progressively more frenetic as his excitement mounts. A clear example of this progression can be found in his references to his wife, Sa-Maria Andreza. He first refers to her as "a good soul but a little past her prime," but as he begins to effervesce he praises her domestic virtues and alludes to her as "well-preserved." She then becomes his "healthy" wife, "betrothed and bestowed on me," then "Sa-Maria my Andreza . . . beautiful and young again," and finally "Sa-Maria darling Andreza." Willi Bolle identifies the rancher himself as a "magic helper" in this story,[6] though as the narrator of his own tale he clearly develops his own persona as much as those of the other characters. Joaquim Norberto's liminality resides in the vague dementia occasioned by the arrival of the message and in his fleeting recapture of youthful ardor, though the transformation is mitigated by its very transience. This rather low-key threshold obtains in only a few of the stories of *PE*, most of them about presumed or self-declared he-men.

In these three stories, liminals marked by their belligerence are key figures, and in each the final transformation turns on unexpected manifestations of character. In "Notorious," events hinge on a theme at least secondarily present in all of Guimarães Rosa's works—the meaning of a word. The story works somewhat less well in English than in the original, because the Portuguese word *famigerado* probably has a somewhat more sinister ring than "notorious." In this story, a bandit chief informs the doctor that a young government man has been going about referring to him as *famigerado*, and he wants to know what the word means. Assured that the word has no pejorative connotations, the bandits ride off. In "The Dagobé Brothers" a similarly threatening situation is unexpectedly defused. Here the liminals are the three formidable brothers of a man murdered by one Liojorge. The expectation of revenge increases when the three uncharacteristically arrange for a funeral for their deceased sibling. Even more surprising is the appearance of Liojorge, whom the brothers immediately conscript as a pallbearer. Virtually all the other characters (and the reader) expect Liojorge to be dispatched at graveside, but instead the brothers admit that their brother was a scoundrel and reveal their intention to move away to the city. One of the dynamic features of this story is that Liojorge appears to the reader to be the threshold being throughout—on the verge of death—and the reversal showing the transformation to be in characters not established as likely candidates for change is a pleasant surprise not just as a plot turn but because it is an artistically appropriate solution. In "My Friend the Fatalist" another rustic is being terrorized by a bully, who has taken a shine to the man's wife and has even followed them when they moved from one town to another. The friend, also a bit on the daffy side, insists that the Greeks, who understood Fate, were right all along. He shows the terrified man his array of weapons and encourages him to take one. He loads a gun himself and follows the man into the street, where the bully is met and liquidated—with two bullets, one of them no doubt redundant.

Read simply as plots, these three stories appear to follow fairly conventional short-story models, and they come the closest of any in the book to having the "surprise ending" of the traditional form. In addition, the thresholds in these narratives are largely dramatic rather than metaphysical, and the transformations which take place, while definitive, are of something less than transcendent importance.

In sharp contrast to this very low threshold construct, three of the stories in *PE* involve marginals who are permanently alienated from their communities. "Sorôco, His Mother, His Daughter," one of the most affecting tales in the book, concerns a man, Sorôco, who has finally decided to send his mad mother and daughter off to an insane asylum. The whole town turns out to wait for the special railroad car the government has sent. Sorôco appears with his two harmless but hopelessly demented relatives, and suddenly the daughter begins to sing a garbled chant. The mother joins in. The train arrives and they are taken away. As he turns to leave, Sorôco himself begins to sing the same meaningless song, ". . . and then, with no agreement beforehand, without anyone's realizing what he was doing, all, with one voice, in their pity for Sorôco, began to accompany that nonsense song" (218). The liminality in this story is not only a permanent condition for the two central threshold characters but is transferred, temporarily, to all the others. Another permanent alien is found in "A Woman of Good Works." This curious tale, narrated in direct address to a plural "you," is about one of the town eccentrics, a crazy woman called Marmalade Mule. The narrator informs his listeners that, although the woman acted as the guide for the repugnant and arrogant blind man Clubfoot, she was really a benefit to the community. He goes on to explain that Clubfoot may have been her son, and that Marmalade Mule had murdered his father and blinded the boy, both deeds worthy of praise, since either of them left to prey on the community would have been worse than any crime. There is also reason to believe that she may have helped Clubfoot along a little when he died. Now, the narrator says, she's dead herself, but just before she died she found a dead dog in the street and carried it off. Why? To prevent illness? Out of pity? For solace? The answer is not, of course, provided, but it would appear that the woman, for all the sordidness of her life, has achieved a kind of grotesque grace foreign to those on this side of the threshold. Perhaps the least "real" of the liminals in *PE* is the character in "A Young Man, Gleaming, White," who appears to have descended to earth aboard a meteorite. Readers of Spanish American fiction will no doubt be reminded of the mysterious types in García Márquez'

"The Handsomest Drowned Man in the World" and "A Very Old
Man With Enormous Wings," who share the otherworldly appearance and uncanny winsomeness of this personage. The young man
appears shortly after an unknown object comes out of the sky caus-
ing an earthquake and flood. Taken in by one of the residents, he is
almost forced into marriage by an irate father who learns that the
young man has placed his hand on his daughter's breast. But the
young man appears to be able to get even the most irascible of
people to like him. He discovers a treasure for the girl's father and
then goes out one night and disappears. After his departure the girl
he touched remains in a permanent state of bliss, and all the others
experience *saudade* and something like death whenever they think
of him. His gleam, it is said, remains.

Two other stories in the book are based on the reader's acceptance of the magical properties of things, but in them the tale hangs
not on the surprise manifestation of an enchanter but on a process of
internalization. In "Substance," a man named Seo Nésio has inherited a manioc plantation. At the behest of an old woman named
Nhatiaga he takes under his care a mysterious girl called Maria
Exita, who has been abandoned by the other members of a bizarre
family—her mother deranged, her father a leper, her brothers mur-
derers. Put to work at the most difficult job, splitting sheets of dried
manioc on stone slabs in the sun, she becomes the focus of Seo
Nésio's progressively obsessive attentions. He worries about possible rivals and starts appearing at the laborers' parties just to watch
her. He finally goes to see her, and the gleaming substance seems to
fuse with the perfect vision of the girl in his mind, driving away all
doubts. The story ends with their shared epiphany of perfect love,
white and complete. The liminality here operates on several levels,
since the substance itself is the ostensible vehicle of revelation, but
the girl herself has many of the characteristics of marginality and the
old woman might be viewed as a magic helper. Also internalized is
the crossing of the threshold in "The Mirror," in which the narrator
directs a long metaphysical thesis about existence to an unheard
listener. The monologue begins with a dense exposition on the function and place of mirrors, reminiscent in tone and content of the
stories of such writers as Jorge Luis Borges. The narrator explains
that one day he happened to glance at two mirrors at once and saw
himself as a horrible, ugly creature. At that point in his life he began
a long inquiry into his image, in which furtive glances and changed

lighting were employed to attempt to change the image. Finally realizing that his "double" was the jaguar, the man settled on not seeing feline features in the mirror as a first step to curing his image problem. After avoiding mirrors for some months, he finally looked in one—and saw nothing. After some years, he looked again and saw a light, the beginning of an image, an intersection of planes and angles which indicated a soul in the process of becoming. The question posed by mirrors, he says, is whether or not one has managed to begin existence, and the answer is an unemphatic "Yes?". Here, though the object itself functions as the vehicle of liminality, the recognition of the threshold and the attempted crossing are carried out within the main character, who, though lacking the marginality usually implied in liminals, has by his own cognitive process placed himself at the edge of a transformation.

The tales in this book are not easily broken into categories to facilitate discussion of groups of stories, because the processes of fiction and the variety of effect make such analysis unmanageable. But it does appear that the axis of effect in all the stories is change, and in every case that change implies the crossing of a threshold. An approach to these twenty-one narratives through analysis of the changes is somewhat entangled due to the various ways in which transformations can legitimately be viewed. Three differing approaches, each having some features in its favor, might center on different aspects of the same problem: the degree of liminality (from testiness to outright madness), the agents of change (from objects to animals to time-space), or the character of the changed state itself (from a fleeting rediscovery of youthful vigor to a transcendence of self). In a number of tales, liminality is most apparent in the distinctive properties of a central character. This is the case of seven stories featuring animals or children or both as instruments of focus, and of five stories featuring either permanent alienation or internalization of threshold perception. Four tales hinge on liminal acts, and the remaining five feature principals characterized by a range of estrangement from simple malevolence to pure lunacy. In every case the importance of the transformation is weighed in terms of an abnormal perception of reality: either that of the threshold being or that of the community itself in regard to that being. And each story hinges on an agent of the change, which may be the same liminal being, but may also be some secondary liminal being, such as an animal. Stories in which animate threshold agents are not present have a physical object as a touchstone or key element in the process. In two cases the object is an abstraction: in "Notorious" it is a word, and in "Soröco" it is a song. "Hocus Psychocus" might be included in the same category, since the vehicle in this story is a play which technically does not exist. Only one story ("No Man, No Woman") features an agent of a nature so abstract as to be almost impossible to identify. Though the story takes place in a house, the object-transmitter here appears to be something like time-space, since the story revolves around a thing not even as concrete as memory, but on the *effort* to remember. The third element in each tale is the state achieved or recognized at the end, which in almost all cases is an unspecified condition of simply being beyond. In most stories it defies precise naming, though progress toward and recognition of this state is the principal source of effect in every tale.

At least two other features of these stories deserve consideration. One is time, which, though it occurs only once as the thematic core of a tale, is of extreme importance in at least half the tales and of implied consequence in all. Rather than a technical device, subject to authorial manipulation for heightened effect, time is of such importance in the book as to be considered one of the general themes of the work. The framing tales of *PE* are in part studies of the fluidity of time. "The Thin Edge of Happiness" concludes with the words, "It was—here now and gone again—happiness." And the final tale, "Treetops," begins with the sentence "It was once upon another time." This story also concludes with a section subtitled "The Moment Out of Time," which ends the story with, "And life was coming toward him." The framing of the volume with two tales in which temporality, though oblique, is of such importance, is a clue to another of the basic processes at work throughout the book. The stories in *PE* are all studies of the transitory, of attempts to seize the moment, or of unexpected visitations of chance. As in Guimarães Rosa's other works, there is here a clear sense of the becoming, the crossing *(travessia)* being as important as the stasis presumed to exist on either end of the movement, though here the tales all take place in the final stage of the crossing so that the becoming itself is emphasized. Stories such as "My Friend the Fatalist," "Cause and Effect," and "Nothingness and the Human Condition" are those in which closing or reaching a destiny is most approximated. But even in these tales the concept of time marching inexorably toward some preordained goal is vitiated by a persistent usage of ambiguous time referents which dislocate the presumed linearity of orderly occurrence. This is a feature of diction almost impossible to translate, and it is probably the most notable weakness of an otherwise excellent English version. In "Nothingness and the Human Condition," for example, the first sentence in Portuguese is a convoluted extrapolation of the ordinary story exposition, in which the narrator appears to deny rather than affirm the historicity of his tale. The English version includes the narrator's subsequent observation that "Each of us lives only his future past," but Aunt Liduína's death comes out occurring "with no warning" instead of "almost suddenly." Another example, of the dozens possible in this extremely time-oriented story, is the English version's phrase "in sin against their common grief," which in the original is "to sin against *saudade.*" *Saudade* is also the principal legacy of another character in *PE*, the gleaming young man. In addition, the song in "Sorôco," the ascension of "The Girl From Beyond," the unendable play in "Hocus Psychocus," the question about beginning existence in "The Mirror," are all symptoms of passage in process. And each manifestation is a temporal marker of threshold.

The other feature worthy of note is the same one which first attracts or repels readers in all of Guimarães Rosa's works: language. Reading any of his books is an activity that takes a little getting used to, and critics note that *PE* is no exception to the general observation that the author writes in a difficult, hyperexpressive style. But use of language in this book is not what might be expected to be the next step in a trajectory of style which could be traced through succeeding stages in the first three works, though critics still suggest that many readers are likely to be driven away from this book because of the eccentric language use.[7] The density of linguistic novelty is so great in this book that some claim to see in it a self-generating affectation, almost as if the author were imitating or even "plagiarizing" his own material.[8] Mary Lou Daniel notes that the stories in *PE* are the densest of all the author's in the frequency of portmanteau words, the use of verbs formed from adjectives, and ("baroque") syntactic inversions, and she views some of the narratives (notably the "Aldacious Navigator") as so affected as to constitute self-parody.[9] There is no question that any discussion of *PE* which ignores style is bound to suffer greatly by that omission, as there is no question that a great deal of what goes on can be analyzed by dicussions of style alone. Even structural analysts admit that the reduction of the tales to the formulas favored by that system is greatly complicated by both the fantastic dimension and by the fact that the *fabula* cannot be adequately rendered without reference to the manner in which it is expressed,[10] implying that, as in the case of *Grande Sertão, fabula* and *sujet* are in many ways inseparable. A full discussion of the kinds of effect produced by language itself could illuminate the book considerably, but in general the manipulation of language seems to have the same ends—among them novelty, surprise, and rhythm—envisioned in earlier works.

The particular linguistic feature of this book which sets it apart from the others is the variety of style and mannerisms which comprise tone. Point of view and implied listener are very important considerations in determining the tone of stories, and each tale in *PE* avails itself of a slightly different set of relationships in determining narrative form, with the result that the narrative voices in the stories have an extraordinary range of types and styles. Some are basically humorous (of the hebephrenic variety in "Much Ado"), some of a mysterious, almost nondirective sort, emanating from an unknown source ("No Man, No Woman"), others of a more or less conventional first person ("The Horse That Drank Beer") or third person ("Aldacious Navigator"). In almost all of them there is a dislocation of point of view or a fluctuating between two or more narrative perspectives, and there is almost always a changed point of view at the threshold. Whatever the stylistic variety, every tale in the book is different from every other one, and the tones range from an almost biblical diction ("A Young Man, Gleaming, White") to a serious, didactic tone ("A Woman of Good Works").

Guimarães Rosa has also provided some clues about the nature and style of each story, by including, in the index, a sort of pictographic resumé of each tale following the title. Included are a number of representational figures such as men on horseback, cattle, birds, and a train. But none is quite what one would imagine to be a visual representation of exactly what goes on in the story, because no resumé is without signs from its own cabala. Benedito Nunes has noted that among the symbols used are the standard signs now used for male (animus) and female (anima)—but he cautions that those characters also symbolize copper and iron.[11] The Brazilian edition also features some very suggestive designs on the book jacket, which readers not familiar with Portuguese might find illustrative after having read the stories in English. Among the objects pictured: a flight of toucans, a man astride a horse which is standing next to a huge question mark, a turkey enclosed in what appears to be a halo, a sphinx, a Star of David. There are also several infinity symbols. In the pictographic index, all the stories in the book save one either begin or end with that symbol.

CHAPTER 5

# Tutaméia: *Anecdotes of Separation*

JOÃO Guimarães Rosa successfully avoided the conventional throughout his literary career. It is thus appropriate that the last book published during his lifetime be his most perplexing. *Tutaméia*[1] was published in 1967, just months before the author's death. The title, typically, is not really a word but a personally streamlined version of the expression *tuta-e-meia*, meaning "trifle." The subtitle of the book is *Terceiras Estórias*, the progression from "first" to "third" possibly being a contrivance to unsettle faithful readers, who might have been momentarily deceived into thinking they had missed an entire volume of his writing. Or perhaps the omission of the "second" stories was meant to indicate a quantum jump in format or style. Most likely, the numerical sequence is merely another way to avoid the cliché, which holds that two, not three, follows one.

Most of the tales in this book were published between 1965 and 1967 in a medical journal called *Pulso*.[2] The book contains forty narratives and four barely nonfictional works called "prefaces." The prefaces in *Tutaméia* have been widely cited as key documents in the study of Guimarães Rosa's works, and indeed one of them contains specifics on the sources of inspiration for several of his most famous tales. More importantly, the prefaces are in some senses a resumé of attitudes, from which a good deal of Guimarães Rosa's artistic philosophy can be extracted. In addition, the prefaces provide some clues, albeit oblique ones, to the reading of *Tutaméia*, a book most readers will find wanting in clues. Some kind of orientation is clearly demanded for an intelligent reading of the third stories, but not one of the same order needed for the first three books—a cosmic perspective, an appreciation for legendary space and the roll and pitch of time, the leisure to examine things at length. Rather what is needed is a further refinement of the sense of imminence found in *Primeiras Estórias,* an appreciation for the significance of fragments and instances, plus a combination of patience and mental agility to read a shorthand now cursive. The book is full of curious little hints, odd revelations, and stories which appear not to end. Many appear not to be "stories" at all, but aphorisms, parables, or arcane anecdotes which might have come from a Zen master rather than a Brazilian doctor. Among the assorted hints are the title itself, the table of contents and index, the epigraphs, and the prefaces. The table of contents lists the forty-four pieces in the sequence in which they appear in the book: a preface, fourteen stories, another preface, eight more stories, a third preface, eleven stories, the final preface, the final seven stories. All these items are in alphabetical order save two—after the item beginning with *J* are items beginning with *G* and *R*—then the alphabetical order is resumed.[3] The epigraph is a quote from Schopenhauer about the "first reading" requiring patience so that the presumed "second reading" reveal things in another light. At the end of the book is an "index for rereading," another quote from Schopenhauer about second readings, and another list of the contents, this time with the prefaces listed separately.

It is in the prefaces that something more substantial than hints is found. The first preface, entitled "Aletria e Hermenêutica" ("Vermicelli and Hermeneutics"), begins as an apparently serious discussion of generic definitions. Guimarães Rosa informs us that the word *estória* (his word for "story") should not be confused with *história* (the word Portuguese speakers had been using all along for both "story" and "history"). An *estória,* he explains, is an anecdote. Unfortunately, the English word "anecdote" has a narrower semantic range than the Portuguese *anedota,* which is commonly used in reference to a short narrative and as a synonym for "joke." Both senses are implied by Guimarães Rosa. The preface continues, liberally laced with illustrative anecdotes and references to the philosophers and propagators of ideas and tales: Hegel's absolute error and Bergson's absolute nothing are connected to the teachings of Zen, the popular joke, and the Perrault brothers. The essay ends with a series of jokes and conundrums. Though a good deal of ground is covered in this preface, the principal areas of inquiry are two: the form and function of the *anedota,* and the manifestations of the abstract, particularly the concept of "nothing." The careful reader will probably extract from this preface sufficient information on the anecdote to prepare him for some of the rather abrupt endings in the following stories, but the sections dealing with abstracts are likely to be fully accessible only to those with an appreciation for the philosophical profundities of the popular joke. This section of the essay is largely metalinguistic—not in the self-conscious structuralist sense (writing about writing), but in the traditional sense of examining a linguistic system's connection to a culture's perceptions of real and unreal. Since "nothing" is an abstraction in both English and Portuguese (that is, not wholly real because it is unmeasurable, invisible, odorless, tasteless, and so on), its "existence" is based on a combination of faith and the elasticity of the linguistic system's codification of real. Three interesting examples of attempts to do this, among the dozens cited in the preface, are the following definitions, the first from a child, the second and third adult explanations of items important in Brazilian culture:

Nothing—"a balloon, without the skin" (6).

A hammock—"a bunch of holes, tied together with string" (10).

Sugar—"a fine white powder which gives a very disagreeable flavor to coffee when you don't put it in" (10).

The second preface is entitled "Hipotrélico," which might easily be rendered as "Hypotrelic," since the word exists in neither language. The subject of this essay is the neologism, and the process is the one Guimarães Rosa used in everything he wrote. The principal illustration for the theory is another anecdote, based on the observation that many words not in common usage are nevertheless derived from "the good Portuguese." This "good Portuguese" turns out, oddly enough, to be not a language but a person. The anecdote recounts that the Portuguese, miffed at a third party, observed to his listener that the person was very "hypotrelic." Informed that the word did not exist, the Portuguese became irritated—if he was using the word, it obviously did exist. When the listener insisted that there was no such word, the good Portuguese administered the final blow: "You're hypotrelic too. *And it came to exist*" (67).

The third preface, "Nós, os Temulentos" ("We, the Drunken"), is a narrative consisting of some two dozen drunk jokes stitched together. Most of the jokes are antiques, and most will be familiar to the reader. Like most drunk jokes, the initial propositions derive from a skewed perception of reality, the revelation of which is the basis of the humor. When discovered struggling in vain with the lock on the outside door of a building, the drunk is asked how he expects to open the locked entrance with a cigar: "Well . . . Then I must have smoked the key" (104).

The final preface, also anecdotal, is "Sôbre a Escôva e a Dúvida" ("On the Brush and Doubt"). The longest and most convoluted of the prefaces, it also covers the broadest range of topics. This preface is divided into seven sections, each dealing with a separate topic: the reciprocal creation of characters (each of us creates characters of our friends, and they do likewise to us); the vastness and impossibility of apparent reality; time; the inadequacy and duplicity of language as a means of communication; the persistence of useless habits (here enters the brush, which is used on the teeth—inexplicably—before breakfast); serendipity (including the revelations about writing earlier works); the illusion of reality. The thread connecting this quilt of ideas is a single concept, found in one form or another in each of the seven sections—a sample from any one of the sections may be applied by extension to all the prefaces. The seventh section of the last preface, for example, departs from the disarmingly simple notion that what we see is wrong—what *is* is something else. It is obvious that Guimarães Rosa meant this to apply to the other sections of his preface as well—that it was necessary to point out that characters, time, words, habits, and the felicitous discoveries of the mind are all interconnected manifestations of illusion, and that what ordinarily passes for reality is, or might just as well be, illusion. Though the first three prefaces place more emphasis on humor (itself dependent for effect on the interplay between reality and illusion), it would appear that absolutes and the words we use to capture those absolutes are in the end dependent for their existence upon a particular perception. Drunkenness is only one of the alternative states of perception—its reality is different but as internally cohesive, as real, as any other.

The prefaces of *Tutaméia* are, then, precisely the opposite of philosophical treatises. Rather than attempts to employ logic and reason in the explication of an orderly system, they are statements on the randomness of all order, expositions on a reality no longer hinged to a coherent system. Given the importance of the tangential, the unexpected, and the extrareal in earlier works, it is not surprising that the prefaces have been used by critics as a point of departure for discussing all of Guimarães Rosa's works. And given the straightforward presentation, it is not surprising that a title such as "Anecdotes of Abstraction" can be applied to a discussion of *Tutaméia*.[4]

Guimarães Rosa himself provides this denomination, on the first page of the first preface. But he also warns repeatedly that nothing is what it appears to be, so it is worth examining a categorization so easily tossed away.

Like the word "hypotrelic," the concept of the abstract is one best defined in terms of what it does not mean. What might Guimarães Rosa have implied by "abstraction"?—simply not concrete? not realistic? not particularistic? not practical? or not literal? All these negations apply to the third stories, and each has application in greater or lesser degree to every story in the book. But, as is the case of any broad generalization, universal applicability is itself a weakness, since in applying to all it tells so little about any one. What is a useful definition of "abstraction," and one which is sufficiently specific to be of interest, is abstraction in the sense of "removal" or "separation." Since there are so many stories in the book, anybody who wishes to talk about the work as a whole is bound to end up inventing a sort of literary scorecard, on which to jot down features which might be shared by all the narratives. On such a scorecard, it might be discovered that most of the stories, perhaps thirty, revolve around a love interest or an interpersonal conflict, much like the stories of *Corpo de Baile*. All but a handful involve some sort of liminality, as in *Primeiras Estórias*. A number are framed in the manner of folktales or at least share features of the folk view and idiom of *Sagarana*. But the similarities are superficial and overly general. One of the few features both applicable to every tale and specific enough to shed some light on the book is the concept of separation. The narratives of *Tutaméia* are uniformly person-centered anecdotes, in which a principal is separated from, or separates himself from, another character. The range of types of separation is great, but the central abstraction is of such importance as to constitute the essence of the bulk of tales.

As in many of the earlier works, death in *Tutaméia* is treated in terms of separation. The consequences of death for those involved in the process are left without comment—death is important to those who stay behind. About three-fourths of the anecdotes deal with an important death, a number of them murders. Most of the remaining tales involve either a physical separation (frequent in the stories about love) or a psychic distancing (akin to the state of separateness of the liminals in the previous volume). In a number of cases, at times in combination with either a death or a love motif, a principal character alienates himself from those around him or is forced into the role of a noncommunicant in the social or family group. Given such a frame of reference, it is obvious that the problem of communication (dealt with in the fourth preface) is a key element in all the stories, and the question of reality/illusion a concept which determines the shape of every anecdote.

One of the very few critical studies on *Tutaméia* with pretensions to completeness is a structuralist analysis which attempts to reduce the narratives of the book to formulas. In this very thorough work, four different patterns are established to describe the narratives, and even then two of the tales are excluded. The base motif is, "The protagonist is beset by a difficulty, threat, or misfortune," and its four corollaries are:

1. His reaction is resignation. He may receive help (nine tales).

2. He reacts with heroic qualities (astuteness, tenacity, strength) and overcomes adversity (ten tales).

3. He retreats into his imagination, hoping that his fantasy will come true (eleven tales).

4. He retreats into his imagination, but reality refuses to bend before the fantasy (eight tales).[5]

As reproductions of the basic *fabula* lines of the tales, this scheme provides an adequate outline of the elements involved in the anecdotes, though it makes the structures appear more conventional than is really the case. In addition, it favors the analysis of motifs over discussion of essential sources of probable reader reaction, providing a problem and one of four possible resolutions (form) rather than dealing with the treatments of motif which provide the reading experience (effect). Given the variety of stories in *Tutaméia*, it would not be surprising to see any general discussion of the volume having recourse to as many as a dozen lines of inquiry. There are, nevertheless, points of convergence along these lines, which, motifs aside, may provide some insight into the workings of most of the stories.

Most of the third stories, though very brief, have a complex enough thematic core to involve at least two or three elements commonly recognized as "themes." Love and death, for instance, among the most traditional themes of world literature, are also

among the most common in *Tutaméia*. Love is a thematic core in
"Orientation," "Story No. 3," "One End Against the Middle," and
"Shorthand," to name only a few. But in each its relative importance
is quite different, and in each the essential effect of the story is
produced not through the traditional unfolding of amorous interest
but through a process which unveils types and degrees of separation. Every story in the book, in fact, can be examined in terms of
this single abstraction. Eighteen of the stories are fundamentally
concerned with the problems of alienation or separation from
people; twenty-two with separation from "reality," which the reader
will keep in mental quotes along with its colleague "illusion" after
having read the prefaces.

In order to avoid the discussion of these tales in a vacuum, each
story has been reduced to the barest synthesis, so that some idea
of each tale's form be available. Naturally these distillations are
somewhat arbitrary, since some of the anecdotes are much more
complex than at first appears to be the case, and all are misleading
by reason of the very degree of condensation. Again, it should be
noted that all tales cross the boundaries of these categories and
might legitimately be included under two or even three of the sub-
divisions.

Separation or alienation from people appears as a major occurrence in a number of stories and in a variety of manifestations. The
following tales seem to be those most clearly concerned with a
process of growing away or removal:

"Arroio-das-Antas" ("Arroyo of the Tapirs")—Drizilda, widowed
at age fifteen, is isolated in a silent village inhabited by old people
until her prince charming arrives.

"Orientação" ("Orientation")—the Chinese Quim leaves his
wife when his marriage fails, leaving behind a woman permanently
prettier because of her Chinese walk.

"Sinhá Secada" ("Mrs. Withered")—A woman's son is taken from
her when she is unfaithful, and she withdraws into semi-isolation.
She comforts a young man looking for his lost mother, and later
discovers her own son died as an infant.

"Desenrêdo" ("Disentanglement")—Jó Joaquim marries an unfaithful woman and expels her from home, but accepts her back after
he has fabricated an unblemished past for her.

"Quadrinho de estória" ("Sketch of a Story")—A young man in

prison ruminates on life, love, and liberty when he sees a woman in blue pass by.

"Lá, nas campinas" ("Out There in the Country")—A man obsessed with his scarcely remembered youth in the country succeeds materially but gets into amorous difficulties, reacting under pressure with a fragment of a long-remembered sentence.

"Mechéu" ("Mechéu")—the idiot Mechéu withdraws into himself when his only friend is killed by a steer.

"Barra da Vaca" ("Cow Narrows")—Jeromoavo, hated by his wife and children, leaves to roam the world and settles in a small village. He is expelled from town when the rumor that he is a bandit spreads.

Several different kinds and degrees of alienation are apparent in this group of tales, but in each the process of losing communication with others is an essential part of the narrative's effect. Isolation may be voluntary or semivoluntary, as it is in "Arroyo of the Tapirs," "Orientation," "Mrs. Withered," and "Disentanglement." It may be altogether involuntary, as the case of the prisoner in "Sketch of a Story." In two stories alienation approaches the psychological definition of the term ("Out There in the Country" and "Mechéu"), and in the final story ("Cow Narrows") at least two separate instances of isolation are implied, one voluntary and the other forced. These stories also have several other strong thematic undercurrents: all eight include love (fraternal or sexual, failed or successful) as a principal axis, at least three of them deal with the abstract state of *saudade,* and four are directly concerned with death. But each plot turns on the process of a character's distancing himself or being distanced from those around him, and each focuses on the space— the nothing—which separates one character from another.

Death, which is a turning point in half these stories, is the central component in another large group of tales. As the most extreme step in the process of distancing, death in the specific form of murder seems to appear as a sort of last recourse in characters' persistent ambition to be alone. Ten stories are essentially concerned with death, sometimes violent, as a metaphor for the ultimate withdrawal:

"Êsses Lopes" ("Those Lopes Men")—The female narrator marries and eliminates the Lopes men one by one and ends up prosperous—and alone.

"Uai, eu?" ("Who, Me?")—The narrator murders three men he thinks are threatening his patron.

"Intruge-se" ("Fool Yourself")—Ladislau solves the murder of one of his men.

"Estória n. °3" ("Story No. 3")—Joãoquerque becomes surprisingly courageous and kills the bully who he thinks is threatening his intended.

"Estoriinha" ("Little Story")—Two rivals see their girl friend arrive. She kills one, and the other resolves to follow her, even to prison.

"Azo de almirante" ("Admiral's Opportunity")—Hetério spends several years helping others, but loses his family and finally his life in the process.

"Como ataca a sucuri" ("How the Anaconda Attacks")—Drepes, a traveler, outwits the sinister Pajão.

"Antiperipléia" ("Antiperiplus")—A drunken guide possibly murders his blind patron.

"Droenha" ("Droenha")—Jenzirico flees to the hills after killing a man, is beset by guilt and fear until he learns that the man died at another's hand.

"Vida ensinada" ("Educated Life")—Serafim takes over both the wife and the job of his murdered companion.

The central preoccupation with murder as a form of alienation is most obvious in the two tales with serial homicides ("Those Lopes Men" and "Who, Me?"), and in one tale in which both the exposition and the climax hinge on a murder ("Fool Yourself"). In both "Story No. 3" and "Little Story" murder is construed by the protagonists as an impediment-clearing device in amorous relationships, while in two others ("Admiral's Opportunity" and "How the Anaconda Attacks") death, though central to the narrative process, is viewed in a rather more philosophical light as a natural accident which just happens to remove its victims from the scene. The final three stories in this group ("Antiperiplus," "Droenha," and "Educated Life") are interesting examples of the combination of alienation-by-murder and alienation from reality, since in the first two it is not even certain who is responsible for the murders and in the third the responsibility and outcome are clouded by doubt. Although some of these stories are reminiscent of certain of the scenarios of violence seen in earlier Guimarães Rosa pieces, and in most there is either a murder or an attempted murder, the process of dying as absence, as withdrawal, persists. In those tales in which there is doubt about the circumstances of death, there is a clear connection with the next group of tales, in which notions of reality and illusion constitute the base perspective of the narrations.

In this group of tales, alienation and withdrawal are viewed as basically a product of individual or collective perception, the distance between characters being lengthened or shortened by fluctuations in the mind's eye. In some, changes of reality are wrought by acts of will; in others, the inability of characters to view the world in an alternate light determines the configuration of the real:

"A vela ao diabo" ("One End Against the Middle")—Separated from his lover, Teresinho alternately indulges in suffering, prayer, and deception, but he finally marries the girl.

"Se eu seria personagem" ("If I Were a Character")—The narrator points out a girl he admires to a friend, and almost loses her to him.

"Sota e barla" ("A Luff and a Lee")—Doriano races to get his herd of cattle home first while keeping two girl friends on the string.

"João Porém, o criador de perus" ("John But, Turkey Farmer")—John, a successful turkey farmer, falls in love with a girl invented by his friends, but she "dies" when he refuses to seek her out.

"Reminisção" ("Remembrance")—Romão forgives his wife both her infidelity and her ugliness because of the way he sees her.

"Palhaço da bôca verde" ("The Clown With the Green Mouth")—A retired circus clown searches for his lost lover, then dies together with the prostitute who knew her.

"Os três homens e o boi dos tres homens que inventaram um boi" ("The Three Men and the Steer of the Three Men who Invented a Steer")—Three cowboys invent a marvelous tale of a steer, and the sole survivor of the group hears the yarn years later.

"Rebimba, o bom" ("Rebimba the Good")—The narrator finally searches out a mysterious benefactor, reaching him just in time for the funeral.

"Retrato de cavalo" ("Portrait of a Horse")—A photo of a horse and a girl is coveted by the horse's owner and the girl's boy friend. The horse dies and the girl leaves, and the photo loses its appeal.

"Umas formas" ("Shapes")—A priest attempts an exorcism and ends up exorcised.

"Tapiiraiauara" ("Tapir Hunt")—The narrator tricks Isnar into missing an easy shot at a tapir.

"O outro ou o outro" ("The Other or the Other")—The narrator and his uncle go to a Gypsy encampment to question a man, who conceals his profession but returns stolen goods.

"Zingarêsca" ("Gypsy Story")—A group of Gypsies deceives a rancher, a blind man, and a dwarf.

"Melim-Meloso" ("Harry Honeytongue")—Anecdotes of a man who always comes out on the better end of any deal.

A number of these tales are framed in entanglements of an essentially amorous nature. The recurring theme of love seems here construed as the most accurate barometer of a kind of index of affection/disaffection. Three stories ("One End Against the Middle," "If I Were a Character," and "A Luff and a Lee") involve both individual perceptions and the importance of accidental unfoldings, whereas another three ("John But," "Remembrance," and "The Clown") are concerned with proximity and distance almost exclusively as products of point of view and attitude.

Another five stories, each with differing processes, expose reality as the exclusive product of the mind: "The Three Men and the Steer," "Rebimba the Good," "Portrait of a Horse," "Shapes," and "Tapir Hunt" all feature entanglements and climaxes which could not have materialized unless a dimension which appears to be literal is displaced by a reality apparently fabricated by the minds of the characters. The invented reality, because it is a product of the mind, is more concrete to its inventors than the literal plane, which remains an alternative unverified by imagination. The last of these tales, "Tapir Hunt," is an interesting example of a story which hinges on a reality created solely by language. The final three tales of this group are stories in which an entire group or community perceives the world not as a manifestation of the visible but as the product of collective belief. Two of these tales feature Gypsies ("The Other or the Other" and "Gypsy Story"), and the last ("Harry Honeytongue") stars a protagonist manufactured along the lines of the North American tall tale hero.

In the final grouping of stories many of the characters are relatively aware of their withdrawal or distancing from their fellows. Several of them are comparable to the "liminals" in *Primeiras Estórias* and in fact one story ("Crossover") is based on a conceptual replica of the title story of the English translation of that volume. These stories are all framed either by voluntary withdrawal toward some third bank or are tales shaped by accidental and sometimes inexplicable discoveries of process. In some of them the term "serendipity" (mentioned in the fourth preface) can be applied:

"Hiato" ("Hiatus")—Two cowboys come across a huge bull loose in the fields, but decide to leave it alone when they realize it's really a tame steer.

"Grande Gedeão" ("Big Gideon")—Hardworking Gideon takes a parable literally and becomes wealthy and successful by giving up work.

"Curtamão" ("Shorthand")—The narrator, a stonemason, builds a house for the lovesick Armininho in order to help him win a bride. The couple elopes and the strange house becomes a government school.

"Faraó e a água do rio" ("Pharoah and the Waters of the River")—A group of Gypsies is hired to repair the sugar cauldrons on a ranch and becomes attached to the rancher's family. When neighbors arrive accusing the Gypsies of theft, the rancher protects them.

"No Prosseguir" ("In Process")—A young jaguar hunter, wounded in a previous hunt, stops by to see his father, also a hunter, and to covet his stepmother, whom it appears he may "inherit."

"Tresaventura" ("Disadventure")—Little Maria Myself, fascinated by rice fields, sets out to see them, but instead saves a toad from a snake.

"Ripuária" ("Crossover")—Melancholy Lioliandro, who seeks solace in a canoe in the river, discovers that the girl who is flirting with him is from the other side.

"Presepe" ("Créche")—Old Uncle Bola, left alone on Christmas Eve, arranges a manger scene with live animals.

In two of these stories, withdrawal from a norm is undertaken consciously. In one ("Hiatus") the result is simply a sense of termination, and in the other ("Big Gideon") the outcome is serendipitous. Three of the tales ("Shorthand," "Pharoah and the Waters of the River," and "In Process") hinge on accidental or unforeseeable developments, and another ("Disadventure") combines marginality of character and distortion of perception, as in the first stories. The final two tales ("Crossover" and "Créche") are easily linked to the same order of threshold perception and differentiation from the group found in those stories of liminality.

*Tutaméia* has probably produced the most varied critical reaction of any of Guimarães Rosa's books. Although at the time of the book's publication the author was generally considered the living master of Brazilian prose, many critics have expressed reservations, either directly or by implication, about this work. Although some writers think the book is one of his best, or at least one of his most interesting for its microcosmic view of his entire work,[6] critics are anything but uniformly enthusiastic about the third stories. One frequent criticism centers around a sense of incompleteness readers may experience in reading some of the tales, as if what was designed as synthesis turned out to have the effect of abruptness. The unexpected rapidity of plot development and the unpredictability of climax are singled out as features which may leave readers up in the air, especially in light of the general atmosphere of the stories, in which nonsense and paradox prevail.[7] Some critics perceive a "decline" in quality in Guimarães Rosa's works at this point, because it is felt by some that the intellectual and linguistic pretension evident in the making of such stories was an indication that the author was attempting to concoct stories which would fulfill the requisites of some theory rather than provide the other satisfactions of fiction.[8] The very number of stories in the volume has been one impediment to inclusive assessments of the work, and the fact that most tales were previously published in periodicals would lend support to the notion that the collection is a "book" only because all the material in it appears between two covers. There is no questioning the breadth of variety in the tales, and there is little doubt that Guimarães Rosa's intentions as a writer had changed, at least in degree, but it does seem apparent that the author did more than alphabetize the titles in conferring a sense of unity and continuity from tale to tale. The very presence of the prefaces should indicate to the reader that some unusual or at least different elements are going to appear in the work, because the author thereby indicates an awareness that some sort of rationale should be provided for the audience, one of the usual reasons for prefaces. The fact that there are four of them scattered throughout the book, and the fact that even taken together they do not go very far in making the rest of the book altogether clear, must be regarded as among the less usual of the justifications for prefacing.

If the reader undertakes the second reading suggested in the epigraphs and pays some attention to the narratives with the prefaces still in mind, certain revelations are bound to take place. The base postulates of the prefaces are applicable to all the narratives: the first preface deals with the concept of the anecdote and the notion of absolute negation, the second with the applicability of the eccentric neologism, the third with skewed perceptions, the fourth with the interchangeability of reality and illusion. The reader is thus offered a theoretical discussion of form and theme, of language and reality, of the act of communication itself, and of perspective. The other implied theme of the prefaces—humor—is more than just an artistic device, since it amounts to a sort of first corollary in the matter of ways of perceiving. Though some of the narratives are humorous, such features as altered reality, distance, and a fondness for contradiction are of more importance in these tales than the jokes themselves.[9]

The "themes" of the third stories are not at all unusual ones: for the most part, the anecdotes in *Tutaméia* cluster around a handful of the most traditional ones in literature. Death, love, reality, and communication among people constitute a list long enough to apply thematically to every story in the book, in fact. Not so traditional are form and manner of presentation. Serendipity, for example, is not one of the traditional "themes," but the degree to which it informs tales "about" something else must be considered, or else the book and the reader both lose by the omission. The substance of the reading experience in this book is not apprehended through an understanding of the themes, but through an appreciation of the nuances of presentation operating in stories on the same apparent subject. Given the importance of human relationships in *Tutaméia*, it is tempting to establish at the subject level the same sort of mental chart of opposites in tension which can be identified in *Corpo de Baile*: alien and nonalien, truth and lie, reality and illusion, love and separation. The same sort of world of doubles was a major feature of *Grande Sertão*, and one story here ("A Luff and a Lee") seems to bear considerable conceptual resemblance to that framework. In most of the stories in *Tutaméia*, however, rather than achieving effect through a heightened sense of tension by the interplay of contradictory forces, Guimarães Rosa seems to favor placing antagonistic views on a plane of coexistence.[10] In addition, such a scheme does not provide an adequate idea of the manner of presentation. Love, like the balloon without the skin, must be defined in terms of itself (that is, the nature of the relationship must be established in order to define the concept by the absence of such a relationship). Rather than simply a negation of separation, then, love may be viewed as implying a form of separation of its own. Love, alienation, separation, and death appear in these stories not as degrees of affiliation along a linear progression of degree but as interconnected types of linkages on a continuum of disarray. Every "love story" in the book is also a story "about" the absence of love, whether that is physical separation, alienation, betrayal, or simply the revelation that what appeared to be love was something else.

The third stories are also presented in a form somewhat grander than the fragment and yet still not quite a short story, which makes the reading more disquieting than usual, since very often the process is over before the reader has had a chance to sort out the information. Though the form itself shares certain characteristics most readers will be familiar with (the format is similar to what is called a "sketch" in English, not altogether different from the Portuguese *crônica*), the reduction is accomplished not by simple economy but by an emphasis on lacunae: the gaps in lives are the substance of the tales, and the expository process contains gaps of its own.

Some clues to a suggested reading are found in the prefaces, but the stories themselves are also replete with interesting hints. Among the most interesting are the innumerable aphorisms which issue forth from characters and narrators throughout the volume. Every story in the book contains at least one such expression, and it is likely that each tale is in some degree framed around a single pithy phrase. The mechanism is not unlike one employed in earlier works, notably *Grande Sertão*, in which the narrator, faced by the enigmatic character of events, frequently fell back on the wisdom of what might have been popular sayings, comforting because of their incantatory and inclusive nature. Luís Costa Lima has noted the frequency of the aphoristic locution in *Tutaméia* and identified three basic forms: (a) those with a phonetic or semantic modification not affecting the (folk) model, (b) those with a plausible popular form, and (c) those clearly of Guimarães Rosa's own invention.[11]

A few selected aphorisms may suffice to give some idea of the close relationship existing between the whole narrative structure and certain apparently incidental locutions. Each aphorism is followed by the title of the story it occurs in and by a note on the speaker and context in which it occurs:

"Blind men run the greatest risks on moonlit nights . . . " (15). "Antiperiplus"—the drunken narrator is justifying to the listener his role in the apparent murder of the blind man.

"Happiness is found only during the times you're heedless" (29). "Cow Narrows"—Domenha, who runs the boarding house, is talking to the newly arrived Jeremoavo, who has left his family.

"Courage also requires practice" (62). "Hiatus"—the old cowboy Nhácio is trying to decide whether to chase the wild bull or not.

"It's never cold in a nest" (84). "Out There in the Country"—the narrator comments on Drujimiro's attempt to recapture his infancy.

"People also need to be harassed by others" (119). "Crèche"—the narrator comments on Tio Bola's being left alone at the ranch.

Some stories contain a large number of such phrases ("If I Were a Character," for example, has at least thirteen), but in most cases the aphorisms in a single story are all of the same general nature or point to solutions of the same problem. It is interesting to note that, once the story has been read, a particular aphorism may stand as a metaphorical statement of the entire narrative, a resumé which may say more about the tale than the best plot summary. Noteworthy also is the aphoristic density of the prefaces themselves, which might be taken as another indication of the consistency of approach in the book. The frequent use of such sayings has several effects. Among other things, it confers an eccentric tonal quality and establishes an indirect narrator-reader relationship which stems from the persistent affectation of editorial presence. It does appear that the entire work was confected, consciously or not, by a mind at work on the expressivity of reduction, as if to test the adage that saying less is saying more. In addition, some stories seem to have almost no pretense of fictionalization ("Harry Honeytongue" looks as if it might be based on the field notes of an oral folklorist), and some (for example, "Hiatus") seem to be antiplot pieces centered on the absence of events. In all of them, however, the impressionistic prose is enough to sustain the essence of fiction even though plot and structure appear to derive from no known genre.

Whether or not this is an entirely satisfactory procedure for most readers is doubtful. The flight from logic, the terseness of style, and the very difficulty in apprehending the suggestive referents in the work disqualify the tales as light reading. And since separation is an undercurrent of such persistence, many readers will no doubt find many of the stories slightly depressing. But the book is another one rich in humor, originality, and suggestive range, and many readers will find the hard going worth the effort.

CHAPTER 6

# Estas Estórias: *Telling as Living*

IN 1969, two years to the month after the death of Guimarães
Rosa, the first of his two posthumous works was released. *Estas
Estórias*[1] was in the process of being organized as a book before the
author died: the title had been chosen, most of the tales edited, and
at least two different indexes had been drafted. The stories in this
book have an odd and intriguing history, and the exact stage of
readiness for publication can only be guessed at for four of the tales.
One of these, "Evil Beast," was apparently one of the stories
Guimarães Rosa eliminated from his 1938 collection of stories before
submitting the remainder for publication as *Sagarana*.[2] One, the
"interview-portrait" narrative "With Cowboy Mariano," was published in a noncommercial limited edition in 1952, and three others
("The Captain's Donkey," "My Uncle the Jaguar," and "The Man
With the Snare") appeared between 1960 and 1962 in the Brazilian
magazine *Senhor*. Yet another ("The Transient Hats") appeared in
1964 as a chapter in a collaborative work called *Os Sete Pecados
Capitais (The Seven Deadly Sins)*.[3]

Given Guimarães Rosa's almost universally accepted position as
the national master of his craft, and given the generally high quality
of the narratives in *Estas Estórias*, it is curious that the book attracted as little critical attention as it did. Well into the 1970s, in
fact, the continued fascination with Guimarães Rosa as the
touchstone figure in national letters is still centered on his only
novel, *Grande Sertão*. I have alluded to the novel as an extremely
ambitious work, and it is probable that the book's very inclusiveness
is at the heart of the magnetic appeal it seems to enjoy in critical
circles. But except for the epic quality and the dramatic backlands
setting, *Estas Estórias* probably contains as much of the essential
Guimarães Rosa as any other work he wrote. It is an uneven work,
lacking the persistent charm of *Sagarana*, the symphonic cohesion

125

of *Corpo de Baile*, and the suggestive density of *Primeiras Estórias* and *Tutaméia*. It is worth remembering, however, that all those books have a certain unevenness, because every story Guimarães Rosa published went beyond the confines of orderly classifications, a fact which lends a nice futility to schemes of labeling. This book is also notable because in it there are so many features which have been identified as characteristic of one or another of his earlier stories. Unlike *Tutaméia*, which is often regarded as a summa of his work, it is nevertheless another volume which includes many of the elements of a highly individualized and ambitious poetics of fiction. And since the works in it were germinated over a period of almost thirty years, it is probably a more accurate, if less flattering, sampler of the whole of the works than any other single volume.

If *Estas Estórias* is situated in sequence on a trajectory of the complete works, even a superficial look at it and its predecessors reveals an interesting shift in form. *Primeiras Estórias*, *Tutaméia*, and *Estas Estórias* all approach two hundred pages of text. The first represents Guimarães Rosa's first experiment with reduction, containing twenty-one narratives. The second, containing forty-four, is a distillation of a reduction. But *Estas Estórias* contains only nine tales, making the units, in bulk, appear closer to those of *Sagarana* than to those of the immediate predecessors. It is obvious that by the time these tales were in the process of being shaped into a book, Guimarães Rosa had the comfort of a guaranteed audience and little pressure to publish tales of a particular format. Given that liberty, it is interesting that the form he chose resembles in so many ways that of his first published stories, for they share with the tales of *Sagarana*, besides length, certain features of pace, tone, and a sense of narrative gusto which by some criteria would be considered old-fashioned. It is fruitless to speculate whether he thought the experiment in reduction had failed or had merely produced all it could—at any rate, these stories are at least in a formal sense more easily compared to his earlier works than to the later ones.

In addition, the book appears to be somewhat out of phase if placed in a context of national letters. If a trend can be identified in the fiction of Brazil in the sixties, it is toward the ever more inclusive novel and the ever more elliptical short story, both of which Guimarães Rosa himself was no doubt in part responsible. His choice of form in this book, characteristically, turns out to be not a compromise but a negation of these directions in fiction, since it borrows from the short story only the precision of expression, not the narrative aloofness; it takes from the novel the expansiveness of form, not the thematic exhaustiveness. Another feature of these stories, also one which relates more easily to the novel than to the short story, is the combination of urgency and release found in the act of telling itself. One conceit related to this is the opposition *história/estória*, from the first preface of *Tutaméia*, in which Guimarães Rosa suggests that the tale and the telling of the tale are two separate and perhaps even unrelated phenomena—the tale told *(estória)* is autonomous, and it enjoys an immunity from the extraneous verification of the history *(história)* behind it.

A clear indication of the importance of telling is that only one tale in the book has the appearance of conventional third-person "historical" narration, and it is disguised as an unfinished "picture" rather than a story. Four of the nine tales have a fictitious first-person narrator as the sole source of information, two have a combination of first-and third-person narrators, and the remaining two have rhetorically inserted first-person narrators. Those closest to the linearity of historical narrative are among the four not given the author's final editorial touches, and it could be advanced that had they received that last polishing they might have lost some of that historicity and gained some of the falsehood which characterizes the other tales. "Gained" is accurate, because the narrators in these tales take great delight in making obvious the artificiality of narrative and the inaccuracy of the events recounted. The two tales which best exemplify the "man at play" *(homo ludens)* notion behind narration as a self-justifying end are the first two in the book, "A Simples e Exata Estória do Burrinho do Comandante" ("The Simple and Exact Tale of the Captain's Little Donkey") and "Os Chapéus Transeuntes" ("The Transient Hats"). Readers of Brazilian fiction will surely be reminded of two other stories when they read the first tale—because of the donkey, described as having a "paradoxical aura of intelligence," they will no doubt be reminded of the little dust-brown donkey of *Sagarana*; because of the captain, an engaging and literate old seadog who tells his bizarre yarn with a wry delight, of Vasco Moscoso de Aragão, from Jorge Amado's *Os Velhos Marinheiros (Home is the Sailor)*.

The events of the tale itself are unraveled with great leisure, as the narrator recounts a meeting he once had with the captain. Then the captain takes over, and the rest of the tale is his first-person recollection. "On an almost imagined day," he tells us, his ship was called north to the state of Maranhão. The destroyer under his command was called to dock at the port of São Luís to help thwart a potential civil disorder thought likely because of the presence of the Prestes Column in the interior. The narration includes long descriptions of the ship and sailing life and a large amount of maritime lore, among which are interspersed appropriate aphorisms and observations on life. The political situation becomes very tense, and in the middle of the confusion a ship loaded with donkeys comes in for repairs. By a series of mishaps, the donkeys escape. The crew of the destroyer rescues one and claims rights of salvage, and the resolution of the political situation, told in a single sentence, ends the tale.

Guimarães Rosa's sense of play is very clear in this story. The tale belies both qualifiers in its title, since it is neither "simple" nor "exact," and it has the same misleading tempo as the donkey story from *Sagarana*. Like that story, only a small fraction of the narration (six of twenty-seven chapters) has anything to do with the donkey which occupies the title role. Also similar is the importance of tone, as much of reader experience here derives from "listening" to the manipulated monologue of a naval captain who keeps pointing out that he "has his humanities" and then citing Camões or Homer to prove it. The captain (who is the narrator of second degree) takes his time about getting around to the ostensible subject of the tale, though he frequently apologizes for his ramblings and promises to get back to the story. By the time he does reach the central (and climactic) episode, the reader is fully involved in another developing story line, this one political. As in "The Little Dust-Brown Donkey," the crossing of the two narrative lines is what makes the story, and again what appears to be a story about animals is a story partly about animals and partly about something else. It is mathematically impossible to add donkey plus natural disaster or donkey plus politics, but in both cases the result is that the story is an irony about ironies, since, of all the expected things, only the sodden climactic donkey (one an instrument of fate, one a mascot) was not in the calculations. In both tales a creature presented as inherently paradoxical is the vehicle for a foray into the incongruities of life.

"The Captain's Donkey," however, is far removed geographically and linguistically from the *sertão* which is the setting and the linguistic source for *Sagarana*. In addition, the form, with the captain as narrator, affords less room for the mystical and more for the speculative. The captain is a curious combination of pragmatist and dreamer, and his engaging presence obviously functions at the service of an ambiguity previously furnished from folk sources. His diction is a maritime version of Riobaldo's: his observation that "we navigate through life served by cross-eyed beacons" (11) might be taken as a nautical version of "living is a dangerous business." But the general quality of his diction reflects less a sense of urgency than one of pleasure. He tells his story not to exorcise his devils but for the pure joy of telling. Some of his phraseology is composed of linguistic "finds," and he seems to delight in trying them out for effect at every turn. He calls his destroyer a "tin can" *(lata)*, as is done in English but not in Portuguese, which works metaphorically but loses something without the bilingual connection. Something which takes place rapidly happens "in the winking of an oyster" ("num abrir e fechar de ostra," the last word taking the place of the *olho*—"eye"—of the cliché), a mixed metaphor in translation but a gem in Portuguese.

Very similar in conception is the second story, "The Transient Hats." The *sertão* is absent as a source of mystery, the folk residue is minimal, and the story, without the history, stands as its own reason for being. The narrator is again a character, but this time the first-person character remains within the action throughout. This is the tale which first appeared in *The Seven Deadly Sins*, the sin in question here being Pride. The narrator informs us that a very large extended family has been brought together to witness the death of "Grandpa the Baron," the patriarch of the family, described as the story opens as being "on his next-to-the-last legs." Among those gathered for the event are the narrator's father and an Uncle Nestor, who become antagonists in the matter of carrying out the specifications of the Baron's will. The Baron, it seems, was many years before alienated from his wife, Granny Olegária, who once committed some minor affront and was ever after shunned by the Baron. So absolute was the Baron's pride that he had the house divided in half by a wall, and when communication became necessary the two would stand before each other's portrait and address the picture instead of the person. To guarantee that the affront would never be forgiven, the Baron has ordered himself buried not in the regular cemetery, where Olegária has been buried for years, but in the pauper's cemetery, where slaves and other undesirables lie. Uncle

Nestor takes great offense at this erosion of family propriety, and his pique grows to outrage when he sees the motto over the gates of the poor man's resting place: "Return to the dust, wretch, return to the clay from which God made you!" The narrator enters into an alliance with Uncle Nestor, less by reason of sympathy with his views than for his having sired the charming Cousin Drina, and as the funeral cortege reaches the cemetery only these three refuse to pass the gates. But at the climactic moment a servant called both Ratapulgo ("Ratflea") and Bugubú (probably derived from the English "bugaboo") appears carrying the Baron's handsome chamber pot (with a blue eye painted in the bottom) and obliterates the offending phrase with red paint.

There is again an undisguised relish in the telling of the tale, and again the reader's response is likely to depend on his appreciation for the bizarre tale itself and for the diction in which it is related. Many readers will no doubt be reminded of Gabriel García Márquez when they read this story. Reader response to *A Hundred Years of Solitude,* for example, is by no means uniform, and it would seem that one of the reasons for this is related to the degree of each reader's appreciation for the language/story relationship, which reaches the page as a story of hyperbolic decadence related by a narrator whose face seems only at times implausibly straight. The resultant "history" is not easily accepted as real by the literal mind nor is the "story" easily apprehended as a sequence of causes and effects. In Guimarães Rosa's story, the narrator's introduction of his extended family is a minor example:

Yes, all the children born or had by Granny Olegária and Grandpa the Baron, excepting therefore only my Uncle Osório Nelsonino Herval, poet and moneylender, and said to suffer from new and encyclical melancholy, but now virtuously defunct. Plus the leisured capitalist Bayard Metternich Aristotle, my father; and Uncle Pelopidas Epaminondas, an industrialist; Uncle Nestornestório, a judge; Uncle Noah Archimedes Eneas, Near-chineas, or Nó, in the trivial shortened form, a congressman. As well as the aunts Amélia Isabel Carlota, a demented old maid; Clotilde de Vaux Penthisileia, widow of Admiral Antipeace; Cornelia Victoria Hermengard, with her husband, Jonathan Gession, without a profession; and Theresa Leopoldina Christine, who ran off and married Cicero M. Papayas, nicknamed "Saturnalia." (37)

Such passages (and most of the story) constitute something of an assault on the synapses, in which are juxtaposed the classical, the banal, the burlesque, and the merely implausible. In addition to reacting to the variety of sources and the likely veracity of what goes on, the reader is also bound to react to such a text, at least subliminally, in terms of diction alone. Part of the effect stems from a relish in words themselves, part of it from a sense of play brought out by tempting rhymes or rhythms, and some of it no doubt from the conceit of the magic, and humor, of names. Another level of linguistic "find" is encountered in the infrequent speech of the Baron, a colorful old curmudgeon who gathers his anxious relatives around him to give them his final instructions. "Copulate yourself!" he orders, presumably in the collective, a directive the narrator recognizes as an "impossible imperative" but also a means of "making the dirty word aristocratic."

There is, of course, a less frivolous level to the story, though it is so closely intertwined with the various comic levels it may pass almost unnoticed. The "hats" from the title refer to the ornaments and styles adopted by individuals, and a hat, like a name, is said to "compose the man." The Baron, who insists on dying with his hat on, is thereby giving a clue to his gestalt, much the way he does by building a wall in the house or by using a chamber pot with a blue eye in it. The hats, and therefore the people, are in transit, which gives the narrator the opportunity to make numerous observations about this perplexing journey. "The way we navigate in destiny is naked and in peace" (38), is an unpredictable but coherent variation on the theme of life as a dangerous journey, and it has counterpoints in other asides and rhetorical questions, among them, "Is the humble man the only one who escapes madness?" (50). "The Transient Hats," then, is not just "about" Pride, just as "The Captain's Donkey" is not just about donkeys. It is an incursion into the nature of transience and a speculation on life and death. What is different here is that the medium is essentially a comic one, and the reader may come away from the story with his clearest image that of the outlandish Ratflea, a provincial Igor, dressed in his dolman and white tennis shoes, racing toward the cemetery gates with a chamber pot full of paint balanced on his head. As a hat, to be sure.

Two other stories, though very dissimilar to each other and less humorous than these two tales, share the imperative character of the act of telling as a narrative axis. The first of these, "A Estória do Homem do Pinguelo" ("The Story of the Man with the Snare"), again has echoes of García Márquez, the second, "Páramo" ("Paramo"), of Borges. "The Man With the Snare" appears to be another serendipity story along the lines of several of the narratives of *Tutaméia*. In it, the story is related through what seems to be a dialogue between the narrator (whose words appear in roman type) and his interlocutor (in italics). The interlocutor's comments, though presented as part of a dialogue, also include observations on the narrator's credibility, stage directions, and at one point a long parenthetical aside (in a different italic typeface) on the specific lyrical qualities of individual bird songs, reminiscent of the footnotes and fauna catalogs of *Sagarana* and *Corpo de Baile*. The narrator's first-person discourse concerns a small village in which one of the narrator's acquaintances, a man named Cesarino, owned one of the several general stores. Cesarino is incapable of keeping up with his competition because he spends most of his time either putting on airs or hunting, and he is already in poor financial condition when a flood and subsequent drought threaten to ruin even the prosperous businessmen in town. He despairs, and the narrator and his interlocutor here interject comments concerning the "man with the snare" and announce a second part of the story. The narrator then recounts his chance meeting with the incongruous figure of Mourão, who shows up in the middle of the drought driving six hundred head of cattle through the now arid wastes near the village. The two set out together to buy supplies and end up at Cesarino's store, where Cesarino and Mourão surprisingly decide to "exchange rotten meat for rotten tobacco." Cesarino takes over the cattle herd and reputedly makes a fortune, and Mourão pays off all the debts of the store and even acquires a gas station and a billiard parlor before he dies. The story ends with the narrator and interlocutor exchanging speculations on the meaning of these events.

The story shares with the pseudofolk narratives of *Sagarana* a concern for the telling of the tale and a sort of avuncular preoccupation with the listener's ability to follow the narrative. But here the speculative stratum is (at least ostensibly) internal to the narration rather than external: instead of interrupting the story to ask the listener/reader if he is following, this story has pauses in which two characters (the fictitious narrator and the fictitious interlocutor) engage in dialogue about the significance of things. After the story of Cesarino and Mourão has ended, the narrator observes: "We fabulize—we live. Do you suppose that somebody, in a study, has ever ferreted out the turn-and-spin of all the people in this world of mine? I mean up the mountain or down the river—the whys. Behind the cockeyed the straightened out. But as I was saying. Every place is equal to another place; all time is time. Thus: the things that have happened, don't begin, don't end" (125).

The story must be taken, then, as the most elaborate kind of lie, because despite the protestations of the two fictional storytellers that there is "very little doubt" about what happened, there is no credibility to the "history," because both admit that there arc no beginnings and no endings, and both persist in perjuring themselves to keep the story moving. When the interlocutor interrupts the narrator's justifications with the remark "No pause," he is again lying, because the reader must pause to readjust to the new paragraph and the italics. He pauses. This story is full of the kind of deposition a judge in a court of law would order stricken from the record—it has no legal validity because it is inadmissible, but the jury cannot engage in such selectivity of memory, and the reader cannot pretend that part of the text—his only link with the fiction—is not part of the text. Another indication of the degree of self-justification involved in the fiction is the fact that neither of the dialogists ever tells who the "man with the snare" is, and neither seems to know.

The fiction itself (that is, the *estória*) is both a demonstration of the interchangeability of things and people and another exercise in serendipity. It also contains many resonances of Guimarães Rosa's earlier works. The narrator's observation that "We think we live because we want to, but we live because we have to" (105) is a paraphrase of the third epigraph of "Augusto Matraga's Hour and Turn," and his description of Mourão as "like a little kid—who only takes into consideration the imaginary" is again the Mythical Child—Miguilim in *Corpo de Baile* and the duplicated child of the first and last stories of *Primeiras Estórias*. The feature which dominates this story is nevertheless the telling itself, and the narrator's admission that he was an eyewitness to the events but still cannot make sense of them is the same as Riobaldo's confession that his distortions and fabrications were merely part of the inquiry.

The act of telling as a terminus in itself is a feature shared by all the tales in this book, although in some cases other similarities are more readily apparent. One which shares several features with "The Man With the Snare" is "Paramo." The theme of this story is a

familiar one—death—but the setting is exotic and the tone sub-
dued. The tale has echoes of a number of Spanish-American authors, perhaps in part because of the setting, which is an unnamed
capital in the Andean cordillera. The city is most likely Bogotá,
where Guimarães Rosa, like the protagonist of the story, served as a
diplomat. The two Spanish-American writers most easily brought to
mind are Jorge Luis Borges (because of the mysterious and labyrin-
thine intellectual conceits) and Agustín Yáñez (because of the dense
atmosphere of oppressive anticipation). Like "The Man With the
Snare," this story exists by reason of the projected appearance of an
abstract entity who embodies the collective anxieties of the characters. Here he is the "man with the appearance of a cadaver." Like
the man with the snare, he never actually appears in the story.
Another similarity between the two stories is the narrative design,
though here there is no typographical clue to fluctuating point of
view. "Paramo" is told in an alternating first- and third-person
point of view and in alternating preterite, imperfect, and present
tenses.

The tale begins with an omega sign followed by an epigraph from
Plato suggesting that life is death and death life. The exposition, in
which the speculative abstract tone of Borges is notable, presents
the conceit that all great steps in the life of man are preceded by a
death—not the final Death, but *that* death which accompanies
crises. The story itself concerns a man who has accepted a post in
the Andean city with the foreknowledge that one such death awaited
him there. He contracts a debilitating case of *soroche* (mountain
sickness) and despite medical attention continues to suffer physical
and psychic enervation and to live in a state of constant dread.
Besides insomnia and an inability to breathe, he bursts into tears
without warning and comes to realize that his emotional complexion
is largely characterized by an unfocused feeling of hate. Here, the
narrator interjects three illustrative anecdotes about hate, including
one very similar to the "pride" anecdote about the Baron in "The
Transient Hats." He buys "*a book*," which he feels contains a key to
his dilemma, though he knows he cannot open it yet. One day he
follows a funeral procession down the street and into the cemetery,
weeping as he goes. He finally experiences a sense of relief and
leaves the book in the cemetery, but it is returned to him by one of
the mourners. He opens it and reads, then goes back to the city, to
life and to death.

The story is uncharacteristically morose for Guimarães Rosa, but the ideas which inform it and the manner of presentation are for the most part familiar. One of the oddest features of the tale is that it is complete except for the quotation read by the protagonist in the final moments of the narrative. A space was left, but there was no quotation, and it can only be speculated whether Guimarães Rosa meant to leave the passage entirely cryptic by leaving out the words or whether he had in mind an appropriate phrase. Had he chosen one, it no doubt would have illuminated the tale only in the most oblique way, but it seems possible that he may have meant to force the reader to supply one of his own.

This story is probably one of the most internalized of all of Guimarães Rosa's tales, and it is almost certainly one of his most autobiographical, both for its setting (Bogotá) and for its theme (illness as both a premonition and a foretaste of death). This is another of Guimarães Rosa's "secret self" stories, like "The Mirror" *(Primeiras Estórias)* and "Shapes" *(Tutaméia)*, though only the former has the autobiographical tone. The narrator of "Paramo" notes that "This is the greatest torment: not yet to exist" (190), a notion very similar to the rhetorical question in "The Mirror" about whether or not existence has begun. But it is the proximity of the *estória* to the *história* which strikes the oddest note in this story. As in *Grande Sertão*, the impetus to tell seems to derive from a sense of urgency rather than from a sense of delight, but here it is almost impossible not to identify Guimarães Rosa himself as the narrative voice. This is not to say that the presence of a fictitious narrator necessarily improves a fiction, but there is something to be said in favor of extravagant narration by theatrical characters, since implausibility is better appreciated and easier swallowed when delivered backhand. What dilutes the teller's art in "Paramo" is that the story is told with a straight face and the diction complements rather than contrasts with that seriousness—most of the odd and surprising forms contribute to the heavy atmosphere rather than offering new perspectives or illuminating the fluid nature of things. The most carefully worked features of the tale seem to be the philosophical conceits, the atmosphere, and the mysterious nature of death, but all these have been more suggestively treated by Guimarães Rosa, and "Paramo" by comparison seems a successful but rather conventional exercise.

The idea of the "man with the snare" and the "man with the appearance of a cadaver" has a counterpart in the structuring of two more stories in this book. In neither of them is this odd deterministic form given a name, and in neither of them is the rhetorical design at all experimental. The presence of Fate or Destiny as a narrative determinant and the use of third-person narration may seem strangely old-fashioned in the last long stories by an author held to be such a revolutionary, but even within these rather conventional modes the stories *(estórias)* are unmistakably modern, unmistakably Guimarães Rosa.

"Retábulo de São Nunca" ("The Altarpiece of St. Never") has all the ingredients of an old-style local color story: it is a love story which takes place in a little mining town. The story opens with the incredible news that Ricarda Rolandina, the richest and most beautiful girl in town, is going to get married. It is noted that the townspeople probably do not understand love. The narrator then reveals that "before the real story" there was another one, in which this same perfect damsel was courted by the richest and handsomest young man in the region. Their love, perfect and intense, was thought to be destined to result in an equally perfect marriage. But the lovers quarreled, and the young man, Reisaugusto, rode away and didn't return. At the end of the story the town priest, officiating at mass, pronounces the banns and declares that Ricarda Rolandina intends to marry a Dr. Soande, an outsider. The populace is astonished, and outside the beggar Cristieléison ("Christ have mercy") pronounces that "there will be some doubts."

How this seemingly ordinary plot functions as a fiction is difficult to describe. It is important to consider that it is ostensibly a picture rather than a story, since the epigraph describes it as a "polyptych" which depicts a "haunted love." The title of the story comes not from a protagonist's name or a key incident but from a religious painting, reference to which is made only twice, both times in an almost offhand manner. The painting is a four-paneled relic found in the chapel on the estate of Ricarda Rolandina's family and subsequently transferred to the town church. The only panel still visible depicts two men, back to back, who were clearly designed to compose a single figure, no doubt a saint, though nobody knows which saint. The story itself is subtitled "First Panel," and no mention is made of a second or subsequent one.

Chronologically, the beginning of the story is the end, because the bulk of the tale is background for understanding the surprise of the townspeople which is the first incident recounted. This temporal reversal is no doubt designed to create stasis in a story purported to be a (two-dimensional) object. Since a polyptych of four parts is the framing device and the structural model for the tale, it can be assumed that the "panel" shares the two-in-one nature of the saint referred to as "St. Never," and that there are three additional parts to the story, though they are not visible (told). Indeed it is said of the lovers (Ricarda Rolandina and Reisaugusto) that each "must have been born with the portrait of the other within his heart" (203), and that "those who love each other beyond a certain degree should shield themselves against their own thoughts" (201). The saint, now seen as two figures, metaphorically alludes to the two halves of the love interest. The vaguely mythical space in which the story takes place is intended to evoke the perfect chivalric love between the two and also to suggest the temporal and affective distance of the episode from literal truth and present time. The ambiguous remark at the end, after the banns are read for Ricarda Rolandina and Dr. Soande—that "the bells do not toll for love renewed"—may suggest that Reisaugusto has passed from the picture and Ricarda Rolandina has embarked on a new amorous relationship, but it also suggests that the true love has reached a second flourishing, which would be the subject of the second panel. At least six passages in the narrative foreshadow the apparently tragic end of the love story, much in the way details of a painting would help to complete the scene depicted. But the fact that the frame for the story is the dual figure of "St. Never," the doubts expressed by the beggar (who follows the model of the prescient madmen in Guimarães Rosa), the "renewed love" of the denouement, and the suggestion that this is only the first fourth of a longer story all point to intentions beyond those associated with the usual story of ill-fated love. The story, though incomplete, is enough, and even though no one can know the rest of it, it should be told.

The other story with an apparent Fate/Destiny determinant is "O Dar das Pedras Brilhantes" ("The Appearance of the Shiny Stones"). The tale has a superficial appearance of historical fiction, since it deals with the discovery of diamond fields in Mato Grosso, but the characters and situations are all obviously invented. The dynamics of the story turn on the arrival of a group of soldiers commanded by a "Senator" Tassara at a ranch owned by the protagonist's uncle. The nephew, Pinho Pimentel, is enticed partly by the tales he hears and partly by his own cupidity to accompany the Senator on a trip to the diamond fields, where the Senator intends to forestall a war be-

tween two rival groups of fortune hunters. The Senator, also referred to simply as "the Citizen," suffers from rapidly declining health,
and by the time they have visited the two antagonist's encamp-
ments, he has become thin and yellow. During a meeting with one
of the groups, the Citizen reveals that the intriguing little case he
carries with him all the time contains a life-supporting medicine,
and that he has just broken the remaining ampules. He dies the next
day, leaving instructions for Pinho Pimentel to assume command.
Faced with the near certainty of a war and the probability that he
will be killed if he tries to interfere, Pinho rises and says, "In the
name of law and . . . "

This story has most of the earmarks of the tale of destiny, and
Pinho's ascension to the occasion at the end has the flavor of the
conventional revelation-of-courage story. As in the case of Augusto
Matraga, in fact, the protagonist's name changes in the last paragraph (from Pinho to César), indicating his transformation into a
hero. There are also numerous references in the text to the strange
workings of the world. "The world never changes; it only gets worse
from one hour to the next," and "Every lesson is at first a kind of
trap" (217, 230), are foreshadowings modeled on those of the hero
tale. But the figure of the protagonist, especially at the denouement, is an ambiguous one, and rather than rising to the occasion he
seems to descend to it. It is possible to view his final act as proof that
the quality we normally refer to as heroism consists principally of a
lack of alternatives. Since there is no dramatic denouement, the
reader is left to consider the several possible consequences of
Pinho's daring act, which include murder and war—or the triumph
of law, order, and Pinho Pimentel—or even apathy. Support for
such an open-ended reading can be found in the rhetorical design of
the story, which appears to be third-person omniscient narration
but is in fact free indirect discourse, with Pinho's elaborate and at
times pathological thought train intertwined with the narrator's recounting of events. Pinho's mind is a clutter of contradictory ambitions, involving mostly women, diamonds, and his own safety, in
more or less equal amounts. At the climax, his only means of defense consists of an unloaded automatic pistol he acquired from the
deceased Citizen.

On the most serious level, this story could be taken as another
chapter on the deadly sins, since most of the characters and dramatic conflicts are motivated by greed. But the structure of the tale

requires that two contradictory denouements be proposed—one with Pinho Pimentel dying in the name of law and order, the other with Pinho Pimentel imposing that order to his own considerable benefit. The least heroic denouement is a third possibility, with the diamond miners simply ignoring him, but even in that case he would emerge with his skin, probably adequate recompense for a man in such a situation. "The Appearance of the Shiny Stones" is thus a destiny story in the most oblique way. It is a story of the "secret self," since the protagonist's motives are not entirely explicit, but the attentive reader will no doubt consider both the probable and improbable outcomes, which is from the point of view of both author and reader part of the fun.

The two remaining "fictitious" items in the book are both animal stories, both concerned with death, and both based on the notion of dualities of existence. Paulo Rónai claims that "Bicho Mau" ("Evil Beast") was one of the stories cut from the 1938 version of *Sagarana*, and it appears in *Estas Estórias* as one of the stories which did not receive the author's "final touch."[4] The story probably comes the closest of any tale in the volume to traditional regionalistic fiction, and it can even be read as a "message" story about the crippling persistence of superstition in Brazil's rural populace. It opens with a long and somewhat chilling description of a rattlesnake which has just emerged from hibernation. The exposition is followed by a fairly conventional introduction to the human characters, who are hoeing a field. The snake settles down by the water bucket, and the reader's attention narrows from an interest in what will happen to a choice of victims, it being obvious that one of them will be bitten. The snake strikes, twice, and young Quincas, son of the plantation owner, falls to the ground. Carried to a nearby house, he receives the attention of a healer, but his pregnant wife insists that he receive medical attention. Quincas' brother, unable to get the doctor, returns with several vials of antivenom. The plantation owner begins the all-night vigil over his son and finally decides to follow the healer's instructions—he breaks the vials of serum against the wall. The boy of course dies, and his widow gives birth to a dead baby the next day.

The section in which the snake is depicted emerging from hibernation is a masterful piece of descriptive personification, the suspense component is well-wrought, and the climax is both conceptually and dramatically effective—but by comparison to Guimarães Rosa's other fiction it pales by its very lack of ambition. The story does, however, achieve effect in part through the contradictory nature of its parts, a feature somewhat occluded by the seeming linearity of the action and apparent predominance of "what happens" over how it happens. The snake, in all its horrible efficiency, is viewed as a cold and terrifying form of living death, but "perhaps necessary." Each of the six potential victims is likewise presented in terms of dualities—for each the narrator provides a reason for dying and for each a reason for living, a device not unlike that used in detective stories, in which each suspect is provided with both a motive and a plausible alibi. The final part of the story comes with layers of irony more elaborate than those characteristic of regionalistic fiction—Quincas, whose reason for dying was his loveless marriage, is provided with a lifesaving medicine by his wife's efforts, and that medicine is denied to him by his adoring father. His reason for living would have been the child, a son, he hopes, but the child is born dead, in accordance with the taboo, which holds that pregnant women should not be mentioned by name in the presence of snakebite victims nor should the word "snake" be pronounced in their presence. Hélio Pólvora also praises this last section for the introduction of fluctuating point of view[5]—the majority of the passage about the vigil is told from what appears to be the vantage point of the boy's father, but the address form is the periphrastic *a gente* ("we"). What makes the story something more interesting than localistic fiction, then, is a combination of technical excellence and the complexity of ironies.

The other animal story is a very curious sort of tropical Gothic, first published in 1961. "Meu Tio o Iauaretê" ("My Uncle the Jaguar") shares with a number of previous works, notably *Grande Sertão*, the form of a somewhat disordered monologue delivered by a rustic to a city-bred listener. Again, the interlocutor's speech is not registered. The narrator is a half-breed jaguar hunter who lives in an implausibly crude jungle shack, and his monologue is a progressive revelation of his animal tendencies. His interlocutor, lost and apparently feverish, seems to realize the threatening nature of his host, because he keeps a revolver in his hand throughout the story. As he drinks his guest's liquor, the narrator offers food (anteater and armadillo) and repeatedly insists that the guest should get some sleep. Most of his narration concerns his deep understanding of jaguars and his eventual decision to stop killing them; he finally provides indications that he thinks of himself as a jaguar. He has, in fact, lost interest in women, preferring the company of a female jaguar he calls Maria-Maria, and he recounts that on several occasions he has experienced strange blackouts from which he recovers drenched in blood. In the closing passages, his threats become more direct, and at the end the guest apparently uses the revolver. The metamorphosis from man to animal is indicated by a final passage in which Portuguese vocabulary is almost completely displaced by Tupi words.[6]

It seems fairly certain that the man does in fact change into a jaguar at the end, and that the other character shoots and kills him. There is, however, no textual proof that the jaguar-man does not carry out his threat to kill his guest, leaving room again for two reader-generated epilogues. But the story has both the lugubrious atmosphere and the suspense aspects of the horror story, and the principal effect is achieved through the unfolding of a condition the reader has been led to suspect true. Critics have also commented on the tale's use of animal viewpoint over human as one of the most effective devices, and one writer indicates that Brazilian readers are likely to react to the story with particular intensity because of the relationship between man and animal in the culture.[7] Even if the reader fails to react to the metamorphosis, he is bound to be intrigued by the elaborate fabulization on which the possible outcomes depend.

The remaining piece of *Estas Estórias* is the "interview-portrait" "Com o Vaqueiro Mariano" ("With Cowboy Mariano"), which is the only work in the book without the appearance of fiction. Inserted as the third item in the work, it is registered in the index as an *entremeio* ("entr'acte"), and is apparently based on the trip Guimarães Rosa made through the interior with a cattle drive in 1952. It was first published in a newspaper, then in a limited edition *separatum*, and then was by the author's instructions included in this book.[8] The "interview" appears to be a report on the author's education at the hands of a cowboy named José Mariano da Silva. The narrator tells how he met Mariano, and there follow three separate accounts: one in which Mariano's own anecdotes are registered, accompanied by the narrator's comments; another in which the narrator describes the sights and sounds of an early rising on the drive and the information on cattle relayed to him by the cowboy; and a final passage recounting several incidents which take place as the two ride together across the pastureland.

Since it appears to lack most of the external paraphernalia of narrative fiction, "With Cowboy Mariano" might be viewed as an unnecessary and perhaps even inappropriate excrescence in a book of stories. But Guimarães Rosa obviously intended a place for this piece in the book, and it is interesting that in both the facsimile indices reproduced in the author's handwriting in the preface, this narrative was placed at the center of the book, with four stories preceding and four following. In a sense, the "interview" might be regarded as a sort of adjunct to the other stories, a gloss on the whole text, in the manner of the prefaces of *Tutaméia*. Since by including those prefaces the author modified the text of the work, the "portrait" of Mariano might then be viewed less as an appendix than as an organic part of the whole. The feature that makes "With Cowboy Mariano" appear out of place is its derived nature—it is presented as an interlude, was probably based on a real adventure in the author's life, and lacks the fictional artifices of plot contrivance and concealment of narrator identity. It looks, then, as if it might be in fact an interview, or at most a journalistic recounting of an autobiographical incident, an *história*.

But "With Cowboy Mariano" also has many elements of *estória*. The most obvious of these is the fact that many of the anecdotes recounted (in quotes) by Mariano are in themselves stories, "fictions within the interview" similar to the fictions within fictions so common in Guimarães Rosa. This is particularly notable in the two long anecdotes in the first part, which both have the unexpected turns of events and care of pace associated with oral literature. A second "fictional" feature is the immediate effect created by the narration, most notably in the second part. Here, Guimarães Rosa indulges again in the unabashed and ornate anthropomorphism which was so important in his early books, and again the effect is produced through distortion of linguistic convention. It is easy to say that these are merely "lyrical" descriptive passages about animals, but again, as in *Sagarana*, the bovine catalogs are complex pieces of linguistic exposition. A cow is no longer just a cow when it has a given name and a quality of voice and attributes of personality, and the reader is constantly forced into accepting both the cowness and the humanity of creatures, much in the way he is forced to accept the eccentricities of human characters. Most of this elaboration is carried out through sensorial channels, by emphasizing and extrapolating from visual and sonorous clues. The calves, it is noted, *mugemem*—"moo and moan." The word is an agglutinate of *mugir* ("to moo") and *gemer* ("to moan"), but the result is not simply economical: the word both confers attributes (humanity and sadness) and intensifies mood. Another interesting agglutinate is a one-word paragraph which is inserted to indicate the breaking of dawn: "Obluz." An apparent combination of *oblíqua* ("oblique") and *luz* ("light"), it is another example, of the literally hundreds possible, of both the hyperexpressiveness and the illusion-creating quality of the diction. The third feature which draws this narrative closer to what is regarded as "fiction" is probably the most important. Even if the work had been written in standard Portuguese without the framing fictions, the transformation of the event into something more than such an event ordinarily implies draws this narrative away from history and toward fiction. Again, possible examples abound, but a single representative one is the final one in the narrative, in which the narrator and Mariano are discussing the incredible ferocity of a pair of small grassland birds (*quero-queros*, "lapwings") which are attacking the two men and their horses for having strayed too close to their concealed nest. Mariano notes that these little creatures are so tenacious in the protection of their nests that they can turn a herd of cattle, so it would be better to go around them and leave them in peace. The narrator concurs. Mariano's final observation, which might in some more conventional reportage involve the territorial imperative or some interesting ornithological insight is, "Yes, sir. That's the way love is" (98). By such distension of perspective, the most particular things are invested with the greatest universal validity, a process just the reverse of that employed in expository writing.

Roberto Simões has criticized this "hurried" narrative as having been written with uncharacteristic carelessness. It is generally regarded as a sort of primitive essay which would later be shaped into *Grande Sertão*.[9] The comparison justifies the negative thrust of such criticism, but it seems odd not to recognize the real merits of the piece on the mistaken assumption that it consists of no more than field notes for a subsequent work.

*Estas Estórias* is Guimarães Rosa's least organic work, no doubt in part because its components were conceived and at least drafted over a period of almost three decades. The fact that four of the narratives had not yet received the author's finishing touches is also responsible for a certain unevenness in the work. But even the least ambitious and least polished of the stories has a technical quality and intensity of effect rarely seen in fiction. Probably the only reason that the book has received as little attention as it has is that it was written by an author who made it a habit to overwhelm his readers with the successive publication of one dazzling volume after another, and this volume failed to overwhelm sufficiently.

Whether or not the volume as a whole is a worthy epilogue to so distinguished a career, the stories in this book are obviously not the product of a talent on the wane, and at least four of them could stand with the best he ever wrote. Most of them reflect the author's obsessive care in making structure and diction function to the advantage of a total effect. All of them contain features now identifiable as those of the essential Guimarães Rosa: a sense of space, timing, irony, and comic effect, a fondness for ambiguity and mystery, and a genius for language. And, though the variety of effects is great from one story to another, they all reflect a reverence for the narrative act itself as an essential to life, which may be the single most important constant in Guimarães Rosa's writing.

The story of the captain's donkey and the story on the transient hats are both tales in which a voluptuous pleasure in telling are fundamental to both the sender and the receiver. The first deals with the bizarre nature of the ordinary and the second with the ordinary nature of the bizarre, but in each there is a clear sense that any incident is better relished, and more interesting, when it is told. Incidents themselves are devoid of truth and only partially satisfying, and the telling is not only fun but also closer to the truth than the "history" it involves. When the narrator of "The Transient Hats" slips into his story the observation "Let's get on with portraying this world of ours the way it should be before it ends" (56), he is betraying both his deceit (the world not as it is but as it should be) and his sense of urgency to fabulize. Likewise, the story of "The Man With the Snare," which by its narrative design is so blatantly unhistorical, begins with the observation (by the first of two fictitious narrators) that "nothing has a precise beginning and absolutely nothing has an end, since everything takes place at a point on a ball" (99), an observation repeatedly brought to the reader in various forms throughout the elaborately fictionalized account. It is also worth remembering that the other narrator's final remarks equate the act of narrating with living. Even "Paramo," which seems to share with the other stories little beyond the "third bank" phenomenon, begins with a scarcely noticeable double exposition: the philosophical problem is expostulated by the anonymous narrator, and then the story begins, but it restarts one paragraph later in the first person. This story also has some of the trappings of the concealed fictions of earlier books (the symbol and the epigraph), and its climax depends on the nonexistent quotation from an unnamed (and perhaps nonexistent) book. The degrees of fictitiousness implied by these features are difficult to measure, but the story shares both the ambiguity and the fabulization component with stories much more obviously rooted in the narrative act.

"The Altarpiece of St. Never" and "The Appearance of the Shiny Stones" derive from the conceit of the narrative imperative in a different manner, since they are both in a sense incomplete. Both take place in a vaguely distant space, one pseudomythic and one ostensibly historical, but both contain commentaries on the artificiality of the events narrated. The altarpiece tale, supposedly only a fragment of a painting, contains reference to the "absurd" nature of the action, and even the central love interest is described as so perfect that it is "perhaps not yet existent" (202). The narrator of this story also prefaces the tale-telling with the observation that "those who do not understand, narrate" (200). The counterpart of this remark in the diamond story is, "that which is excessively real is what appears to be deception and magic" (215).

Even the animal stories, which have some of the most conventional aspects of regionalism, contain elements of this compulsion to fictionalize. "Evil Beast" is the book's oldest and by far the most traditional story, but it manages to transcend the merely informational aspects of the tale of local color partly by technical manipulation. The suspense component and the personification are conventional but carried out with technical skill. The most sophisticated aspect of the story's content is in the elaboration of the duality of characters and events, but the technical device used toward this end is the shift in point of view at the climax, where Nhô de Barros displaces the third-person narrator as the source of information. His monologue constitutes a sort of fabulization, a way of rearranging reality for the benefit of his peace of mind. Though this is a characterization device and a dramatic artifice, it is also a somewhat rudimentary example of how Guimarães Rosa conceived of telling, even in monologue, as the best way to reach a reality more important than that found in the event. In "My Uncle the Jaguar" this aspect of the fiction is likewise obscure but still quite important. The possibility of two denouements likens this story to several others in the book, in which alternative endings or lack of ending indicated emphasis on the fiction. In any literal way, it is quite impossible for this narration to exist, in fact, since if the interlocutor dies there is no way for the story to reach us and if the jaguar-man dies there is no way for him to tell us. But more important than the obscurity of source, not particularly unusual in fiction, is the importance of the narrative act to the narrator, the jaguar-man. He is of course under no constraint to tell anything about himself, so his incriminating account results from a combination of a desire to lull the listener to sleep and an unexplained urge simply to tell. A question such as "If I tell more, do you suppose you'll go to sleep?" (143) has the effect of heightening the suspense and adding to the already sinister characterization of the narrator, but it also is a hint that the act of telling, which caused the story to exist, is in itself an instinctual and inherently pleasurable thing.

Even "With Cowboy Mariano," which in so many ways appears to be slightly out of place in the book, is a fiction justifying itself by being a fiction. The narrator of this apparent "report" tells the reader as much early in the process, when he says to Mariano, "The true part, whatever it is, of your stories you can in no way relate to me. . . . stories do not just come forth from the narrator, rather they create themselves to him; narrating is resisting" (73–74).

The now dated concept that in fiction "showing" is superior to "telling" would not have found a supporter in Guimarães Rosa. Even the "telling" in that conceit implies a narration which tells what happened, recounts "the way it was." Guimarães Rosa preferred to tell, and in addition his stories, even those with apparent "historical" characteristics, are more rooted in a paradoxical "way it wasn't." The story, in every case, takes precedence over the history, and the act of narrating, lies and all, is at last the single imperative of existence. Oddly, fictions rooted in this conceit share something with political fiction, because both derive from a sense of urgency about getting things down, a kind of messianic zeal. But Guimarães Rosa's fiction lacks the political writer's motivation of setting the reader's ideas straight. Just the opposite, in fact—the urgency in *Estas Estórias* derives from the tale itself, and the conceptual intention, which is at any rate secondary, has the effect of making the reader less certain about things rather than more certain. These stories exist by reason of the obvious but widely ignored fact that the story, for both the teller and the listener, is more important than the lesson it may pretend to illustrate, because since the first parable was concocted the telling—the art—was suddenly autonomous and from that moment on no longer in need of any extrinsic justification.

It would be unnecessarily rash to attempt to assign some relative value to these stories in comparison with others by the same author. Some in this book are obviously less well done than others. But they all share a self-consciousness about the narrative act itself as central to the making of the story. No doubt some readers will find this merely precious, but there has always been a certain self-indulgence in a tale-teller's mannerisms of telling. The point, really, is to do it well. Guimarães Rosa did it very well indeed.

### CHAPTER 7

# Ave, Palavra: *The Word Itself*

G UIMARÃES Rosa's last book was published three years after his
death.[1] This final work contains the miscellany of some thirty
years of writing, most of it previously published in newspapers or
magazines. The author had intended for most of these pieces to be
published or republished in such a volume, and the title of the book,
which is literally *Hail, Word*, is his.[2] Eighteen of the fifty-four
pieces in the volume were nevertheless included at the discretion of
the volume's organizer, Paulo Rónai, who notes in the introduction
that the format of *Ave, Palavra* reflects both some guesswork and
some exercise of his own personal preference.[3]

The components of *Ave, Palavra* could be grouped in several
ways, but it is doubtful that any such compartmentalization would
be of much help in illuminating the book as a whole. It is not, in the
usual sense, a "book" at all, in fact. There is no particular reason for
the pieces to appear in this order, except, as the organizer notes, to
provide the variety of length, pace, form, and style that Guimarães
Rosa thought desirable to avoid monotony and keep the reader
alert. This order functions well enough to that end, but only if the
reader goes through the volume from beginning to end. Many readers will sense early that there is no real organizing principle in the
volume other than variety and go ahead and take a random sampling
of the assorted tidbits in the smorgasbord.

In all probability the most avid readers of the book will already be
Guimarães Rosa enthusiasts, though it is conceivable that a first-
time reader might find the book intriguing enough to want to read
more. It is not, however, a good first book to read, because so many
features of it are intensified and better appreciated through an echo
effect. Mannerisms of style, characters, situations, themes—all res-
onate with fragments from earlier works, and neophytes may find
either irritating or impenetrable such things as the catalogs, tales

148

which refuse to end, and assorted incongruities. When the practiced Guimarães Rosa reader reaches the list of "ten animals for a desert island," for example, he is not likely to be surprised at the existence of such a list and he is bound to expect certain choices (cat, dog, firefly) and to react with associative intensity to others (donkey, ox, turkey). A first-time reader may find the whole thing simply bewildering.

Since the volume is composed mainly of "occasional" pieces, and since secondary effects are of such importance in reading it, it would seem pointless to discuss the work in any great detail. It is certainly not a book which opens an entirely new perspective on the craft, as both *Sagarana* and *Grande Sertão* did, nor is it a book which unveils the artist's aesthetic system, as *Tutaméia* did. Oddly enough, it is a book which deserves attention as much for what it lacks as for what it has. *Ave, Palavra* is the sole volume of the complete works elaborated without the fabulization component which is of fundamental importance in all the other books. As the least fictionalized book in the ample repertoire of an author of fiction, it must be considered in a large way unrepresentative of the writer's best efforts. Viewed in another way, however, *Ave, Palavra* can serve as a window into the creative process of a gifted creator, because its very lack of ambition serves to make the machinery more transparent.

It is true that a number of earlier stories are identifiably autobiographical, but in them no distinction can be drawn between a narrative's "true" parts and those invented, and in every case those stories also rely on effects which go far beyond the inherent significance of events themselves. In *Ave, Palavra* very few of the pieces contain the emphatic posture of the artful prevaricator which characterizes all the other works. Less than a half dozen of the items in this book are products of fabulization: the others have either the appearance of memoir or the irregularity and elusiveness of rhapsody.

There is no adequate generalization to give an impression of what it is like to read the book, and analysis of only a few pieces would be misleading. Five selections are in verse, each written under one of Guimarães Rosa's anagrammatic pseudonyms: Soares Guiamar, Meuriss Aragão, Sa Araújo Segrim (twice), Romaguari Sães. Guimarães Rosa invented these poets and then gave each a poetic personality and a personal style, in the manner of the Portuguese poet Fernando Pessoa, who wrote a complete body of poetry for each of his "heteronyms." Seven pieces are rhapsodies on, of all things, zoos, including observations on the characteristics, personalities, and assorted impossibilities of animals. Another kind of bestiary is a survey of the appearance and significance of the donkey and the ass in twenty-six nativity paintings. Another is a rewrite of *Little Red Riding Hood*, several are memoirs of incidents in Guimarães Rosa's diplomatic career, and others are evocations of scenes and characters from the Brazilian interior. The last five, which appear with the subtitle "Gardens and Brooks" ("Jardins e Riachinhos"), are dense poetic depositions on the microcosm of a small stream, remembered from childhood. Some are funny, others almost impenetrable on first reading. There is a long essay in praise of the streetcar, a piece on the almond tree (featuring the poet Carlos Drummond de Andrade), and a discussion of the souls of cities. Matters such as death, *saudade*, the circularity of time, irrationality as an ontological system, love, destiny, and beauty appear repeatedly. Different typefaces are used, time is distorted, and the unexpected almost always takes place. And throughout the volume there are the familiar gem-quality aphorisms.

Since Guimarães Rosa was demonstrably a master storyteller, and since to many readers the story is the thing, it would seem to follow that such a book would be a resounding failure. Yet even without the essential narrative ingredient, most of the items in *Ave, Palavra* succeed in surprising and in pleasing. What makes most of the pieces work is a combination of a persistently unorthodox view of place and event and an expressionistic diction. The process is one deceptive in its simplicity and almost impossible to copy. It requires first that the subject (whether that is a human character, an animal, a place, or an abstraction) be perceived by the writer in a manner out of the ordinary. The skewed perception can be associative, metaphorical, or even analytic. The new angles of the perception are then indicated by the shaping and bending of the words and phrases used in the passage. The final step—which is at once mental, visual, perceptual, and sonorous—is produced in the reader. There is no test for verifying the accuracy of the reproduction—that is, the similarity between the author's perception and the reader's—because multivalence is an intended by-product. Imprecision, however, is not intended, which is why this way of saying the thing is the best and in fact the only way of saying it. Poets have been doing this for a long time; Guimarães Rosa did it in everything he wrote.

Because language is the major source of effect in about half the pieces in the book, the reader may on occasion experience a sense that to go on would be to overindulge, and it is thus fortunate that most items in the volume are very short. Also because of the preeminence of linguistic effect (or effects produced linguistically), readers are likely to be made more aware of the eccentricities of diction than usual, and some will certainly find it excessively affected. But it is not really necessary to approve of those affectations in order to admire their efficacy. Nor is it necessary to like all the pieces in order to admire the book.

A subject resumé, including the one I have just provided, is rendered almost useless by the novelty of perception and language. The experience of reading involves absorbing the ostensible subject matter only in the most oblique way, since it is not the subject itself but the manner in which it is viewed and expressed which initiates the reader's response. In most cases, the agent of distortion is mystical or at least extralogical, as the author consistently reveals his preference for viewing the unexplainable as one of the positive constants of the universe. This impression is conveyed to the reader by the eccentricity (or affectation) of phrase. The first sentence in the book, in a piece entitled "O Mau Humor de Wotan" ("Wotan's Ill Humor"), is "Hans-Helmut Heubel reread the Cabala or the Bible and believed in a plastic and meticulous destiny, retouchable by man" (3). There is irony and ambiguity in the sentence, and it establishes tone and begins the exposition. But the "retouchable" destiny, plastic and meticulous, is not likely to be among the reader's experiences until he reads the passage, and it most certainly is not implied or required by the story's context.

The vaguely incongruous relationship between context and expression gives a better idea of the book's effect than even the fullest thematic catalog, so it is worth listing a few examples for clarification. It should be noted that in the process of converting these samples to English, I have sometimes been forced to render the sense of the phraseology at the expense of the exact configuration of the original, and some will thus appear to be misleadingly prosaic. One piece, for example, carries a title which in English would be "Some Little Engineers." It consists of the author's observation of two birds building a nest. But the title in Portuguese is "Uns Inhos Engenheiros" rather than the standard "Uns Engenheirinhos," the bound diminutive morpheme "-inho" appearing, impossibly, as a word. This is a very minor kind of revision of perception, but the two forms, the standard one and the Guimarães Rosian version, simply do not convey the same thing, and the reader begins his reading with his perception already somewhat awry. In another essay, this one even having a linguistic subject core, Guimarães Rosa recounts his experience with a Brazilian Indian language he became fascinated with. Having transcribed what he took to be a morpheme indicating "color," he investigated further and discovered it was really the word for "blood." His thought then was that the form was metaphorical, with "red" being "blood of the sun," and so on, but this proved false. He was never able to discover the missing piece to the puzzle, but his initial frustration seems to have been displaced by mystical resignation. His conclusion, typically, is neither conclusive nor subject to logical gloss, but it is typical of the perception/diction merger which is at the root of much of the book's effect: "All languages are vestiges of an ancient mystery." A few other examples of context and expression may serve to give a fuller impression:

1. In a travel memoir about the area of Mato Grosso which forms part of the Paraná River floodplain: "From what abyss were we born, did we come? But in the beginning was the desire for beauty. In the beginning was no color" (173).

2. In a highly internalized disquisition on love and time: "Who are you? . . . I am my own lacuna . . ." (162–63).

3. In a diplomatic memoir concerning a Brazilian citizen who was chronically repatriated after stowing away on ships bound for Europe: The man suffered from "distanxiety—the spatial hunger of the suffocated" (215).

4. In a story about a decision in an old folks' home to hold a second Christmas to give the residents something to live for, one woman fell ill on the long-anticipated day, hoping, it is said, that she would "fleetingly awaken the necessary instant, lucid between two deaths, that is, that she be able to receive her offering and gift before continuing" (227).

5. In a memoir about fortune-tellers: "Every human life is destiny in a state of impurity" (228).

6. In a miniaturistic memoir about insects: Beetles, scientifically

incapable of flight, fly "purely out of incompetence and ignorance" (241). And a locust he picks up one day to ask about its insistence on raising such a constant din answers Guimarães Rosa's question, "DON'T YOU THINK LIFE ITSELF IS AN EXAGGERATION?" (244).

It would be a mistake to regard such locutions merely as examples of handsome turns of phrase or fancy writing, since the oddness of phrase is always justified by the novelty of the underlying perception. This diction is, in fact, just the opposite of the belletristic rhetorical model, which often employed elegance of phrase to camouflage poverty of imagination. Guimarães Rosa's language, by contrast, is metaphorical in the best sense of the term, because the focus is revelation rather than decoration. Even in the apparently afictional pieces in this work the medium is highly figurative, which has the effect of distancing every event recounted a step from literality. What results is probably classifiable as "poetic prose" or some other catchall rhetorical term, but something more interesting than mere stylistic grace should be implied, whatever the term used. Most of these pieces lack the theatrical potential of Guimarães Rosa's previous works because they lack a fictitious narrator, the source of much of the engaging extravagance in earlier works. But since the clearest focus is still highly astigmatic and since the diction constantly reinforces the oddness of the view, virtually nothing comes out pictorially real. Which means that even with the usual paraphernalia of fiction stripped away, Guimarães Rosa still manages to concoct his pretty lies—fictions.

*Ave, Palavra* will probably not be remembered as one of Guimarães Rosa's most impressive works, and it is certainly the least appropriate one to read to get an impression of the writer's talents. It is also a book not really made by the writer: as in the case of *Estas Estórias,* we can only guess how it might have come out if the author had lived to give it his sense of organization and his final touches. It is, in fact, something of a hodgepodge, which one Brazilian has criticized for having the appearance of having been composed "from the bottom of a drawer."[4] It is thematically and technically vast, but it has no single element of cohesion, since the pieces of the whole were composed over a period of at least three decades. Finally, most of it is not truly fiction, the craft for which its author was most famous.

A full paragraph of reservations about the book is proably too much, because probably few readers will attempt it without having read at least some of the earlier works; if they have done that, *Ave, Palavra* is not likely to alter their opinion of the writer.

Despite its shortcomings, *Ave, Palavra* is interesting and occasionally even fascinating. Since the story element of earlier works is absent, the major source of effect is language itself. Guimarães Rosa's view of the world as a complex and contradictory place remains intact, and his way of communicating his multivalent vision of that larger world was to expand the code—language—to fit the vision. The result is a diction at once "poetic" and ungrammatical, and the experience of reading is by turns mystifying, illuminating, and even irritating. It is almost never dull. The reader of this book must finally conclude that what has been passing for memoir is really, like Guimarães Rosa's other books, composed of fine lies, fictions. Everything told means more than it should. If it were really true, if this were really the literal reproduction of event, the author would not have used that word, those words. Hail, word.

CHAPTER 8

# Epilogue: An Extravagance
# of Fictions

IN the course of this study, I have attempted to provide at the end of each chapter a brief resumé of points related to the volume under discussion. Since those remarks are in a sense a body of conclusions, it would be redundant merely to restate them here and pretend I was saying something new. But as a means of clarifying what I have tried to communicate, it seems to me useful to depart from a synthesis of those conclusions. That clarification, I should add, is for my own benefit as well as for that of the reader, since, like most of Guimarães Rosa's critics, I have discovered that working with these books yields not a feeling of mastery but a sense of perpetual apprenticeship. There is always a lot to learn.

I have emphasized only a few of the many generalizations which could be made about Guimarães Rosa's prose: he was consistently imaginative enough to outflank both critics and theoreticians, he seems to have been very aware of the reader's alliance with the writer in the making of fiction, and he was continuously experimenting with the ways fiction could be made (whether for his own delight or for the reader's). In *Sagarana* short fiction is given a new vitality not by a thorough revolutionizing of its parts but by resurrecting one of its oldest elements—the concept of story in its essential function as entertainment—and blending that with an array of technical devices (some of them also revived rather than invented). Together, these two elements provide the narrative with the incantatory energy of oral literature and the aesthetic subtleties of high art. In *Corpo de Baile* and *Grande Sertão*, a similar fusion of components traceable to either popular or erudite sources is visible, but the interplay of effects is even more intricate. Both books may be viewed as evidence of the frailty of generic nomenclature, since there are so many components which elude the precise confines of the conventional concepts of short story, novella, and novel. But

155

they still draw vigor from some very traditional sources of reader satisfaction: tension and resolution, naming and making, secrets revealed, recognition, resonance, irony. Both books are also notable for a breadth of suggestive range barely implied by such a list of processes. The potential of this latitude is so great that it includes reader response from the merely confused to the hyperinferential.

*Primeiras Estórias* is further proof, if any is really necessary, of the amplitude of the author's skills. Neither repetition nor predictable modification of earlier narrative norms, the tales in this book really are Guimarães Rosa's (and Brazil's) first *estórias*. In them, the processes of making the fiction are found not in elaboration but in reduction, and the point of departure is less plot sequence and termination than the revelatory power of bizarre perceptions. In *Tutaméia* the reductive process continues, with the narrative core decreasing almost to the point of invisibility. Where in the previous books effects are found in the very lavishness of fiction's suggestivity, the "first stories" derive effect from nuances of the imminent, where things have yet to happen; the "third stories" from anecdote and aphorism, where narrative elaboration has yet to take place. Another odd mutation occurs in *Estas Estórias*, where it becomes evident that theme, source, technique, anecdote, and even language may not always be overriding sources of effect in a tale, because, as is shown differently in *Sagarana*, the story itself (the fiction, the lie) can be made to stand on its own as the base of aesthetic effect, both function and process. Finally, in *Ave, Palavra*, the author's collected short pieces can be taken as a denial even of the preeminence of story—proof that all these elaborations are good but unnecessary, that words alone are the real source of literature's capacity to enlarge the world and our sense of its meaning.

It is a performance replete with contradictions and logical inconsistencies: certain canons of form are violated and other, older ones are enshrined in their place, only to be themselves replaced in the next volume; time and space gratuitously expand and contract; precision of expression produces ambiguity of purpose; truths keep emerging from the lies. Worse, it is all done in a nonexistent, antigrammatical style, which keeps forcing the reader to do more than his share of the work. Finally, each volume affiliates with the other six in a relationship of serial mutation, as if something in the hereditary chain had been omitted. Every book seems to depart from a different concept of story, yet the reader familiar with one of them could perceive the others' kinship by the reading of a single line.

João Guimarães Rosa was not the first gifted Brazilian writer of this century nor the last, but it is fair to say that, like Joyce, his books have had a profound impact on all the subsequent literature in the language. World literature has been greatly enriched by these seven books, and Luso-Brazilian literature will never be the same. I am not certain that I have provided a full sense of that impact in this study, but I would be satisfied to think that, whether or not that point was clear, I have provoked some readers of this to read Guimarães Rosa, if only to prove me wrong.

I have tried to indicate that I feel evangelical fervor about the writer but not about my approach to his work. If reading these books is often perplexing, writing about them is even more so, because precision is difficult to extract from discussions of works of intentional fluidity. The view I propose here is a general one without pretensions of exhaustiveness, and in many cases I have only mentioned other possible avenues of approach without following them.

It would be misleading to imply that all Brazilians have reacted to his books with unqualified ecstasy, or even that his reception in other countries has been altogether enthusiastic. Most Brazilian critics who have reacted negatively to his books have done so because of what they perceive as their excesses: the style is gratuitously ornamented, the prose is unintelligible, the stories are hard to follow. I have given less space to criticism addressed to what his books fail to do, because it is a critical perspective difficult to blend into a general discussion of aesthetic effects. Some critics have taken exception to Guimarães Rosa's works for not exposing such evils as monopoly capitalism or hunger, others because they do not unmask the sociological truth of banditry. I have heard more than one critic refer to *Grande Sertão* as a "reactionary" work, and I can only assume that the opinion is formulated on the same grounds. Since Guimarães Rosa was a militant illogician as a thinker and a magician as a writer, I think he might have reacted to such observations with bemusement, but it is worth mentioning such reservations to provide a somewhat tardy balance and to reiterate my contention that a great deal remains to be done, simply because the books are so pithy.

I have insisted on talking about the pithiness of the works because it seems to me that their author communicated through them an exhaustive and deeply involved humanity. Guimarães Rosa had a philosopher's concern with essential truths, a dreamer's urge to believe in ones he discovered, and a wise man's reluctance to make too much of them. He also had a mystic's vision of the impermanence of systems and a poet's eye for seeing the extraordinary in the humdrum. He had an enchanter's gift of making worlds out of words and the breadth of view to do so as both a miniaturist and as a cosmologist. He regarded the ordinary with disdain, but his horror of the commonplace did not dilute his respect for tradition, and his often grandiose designs as a fabulist never dislodged his sense of awe that things could be as they are. As a writer he can be accused of trying to do too many things, often at once, and of sometimes failing to do what he set out to do. The amazing thing is that he was so often successful in doing it all.

# Notes and References

### Chapter One

1. João Guimarães Rosa, *Sagarana*, 7th ed. (Rio de Janeiro: José Olympio, 1965). The English translation is *Sagarana*, trans. Harriet de Onís (New York: Knopf, 1966). All quotations are from this translation. Page numbers are indicated in the text.

2. Brazilian critics have struggled for some time to find a term which would adequately describe Guimarães Rosa's peculiar form of "regionalism." Tristão de Athayde has called it "transrealism," and Wilson Martins has referred to it as "universal regionalism." See Athayde, "O Transrealismo de Guimarães Rosa," *Meio Século de Presença Literária* (Rio de Janeiro: José Olympio, 1969), pp. 240–42; Martins, "Structural Perspectivism in Guimarães Rosa," *The Brazilian Novel*, ed. Heitor Martins (Bloomington: Indiana University Publications, 1976), p. 61. The best analysis of the phenomenon, in which *Sagarana* is systematically compared to the traditional regionalist novel *A Bagaceira*, appears in a recent study by Nelly Novaes Coelho, "Guimarães Rosa: Um Novo Demiurgo," *Guimarães Rosa: Dois Estudos* (São Paulo: Edições Quíron/INL, 1975), pp. 11–34.

3. Mary L. Daniel, *João Guimarães Rosa: Travessia Literária* (Rio de Janeiro: José Olympio, 1968), p. 70. Franklin de Oliveira, writing in the preface of the English translation of *Sagarana*, claims that the Tupi suffix means "in the manner of." "Introduction: The Epigraphs in Sagarana," p. ix.

4. Fábio Freixeiro, "O Problema do Gênero em *Sagarana*," *Da Razão à Emoção* (São Paulo: Companhia Editora Nacional, 1968), pp. 51–52.

5. Ibid., pp. 55, 65.

6. Ibid., pp. 58, 65–66.

7. Ibid., pp. 62, 66.

8. Daniel, p. 172.

9. Freixeiro, p. 65.

10. Ibid., p. 60.

11. Ibid., p. 63.

12. Ibid., p. 66. Two other writers have, by very different paths, reached

similar conclusions on the character of this mystical substratum and its importance to the narratives in *Sagarana*. Willi Bolle, in *Fórmula e Fábula* (São Paulo: Editora Perspectiva, [1973]), uses a structuralist analysis to conclude that the base "formula" of the tales of *Sagarana* consists of an act of aggression followed by punishment. His chapter on *Sagarana*, pp. 37–63, is entitled "Offense and Sanction." Suzi Frankl Sperber, in her *Caos e Cosmos* (São Paulo: Duas Cidades, 1976), studied the contents of Guimarães Rosa's private library and analyzed the marginal notes to trace the philosophical influences on the author's work. She concludes that *Sagarana* reflects a noteworthy influence of the New Testament (p. 55).

13. Daniel, p. 104.

14. Emir Rodríguez Monegal comments on the attitude of authorial superiority in relation to characters in "A Literary Myth Exploded," *Review* (Winter 1971/Spring, 1972), p. 63. In terms of effect, it would seem a plausible next step to extrapolate a similar author attitude toward the reader, since many of the characters of the authors referred to (Arlt, Borges, Marechal, Cortázar, and Viñas) are reasonably cultured and could be expected to be at least as intelligent as the readers of the books.

*Chapter Two*

1. It could be argued that another such division was created by the Modernists in the twenties, but in fiction, even the monumental creations of these writers had delayed or aborted impact on the national literature. Oswald de Andrade's *Memórias Sentimentais de João Miramar* attracted more attention in the 1964 reedition than it did when first published forty years earlier, and Mário de Andrade's *Macunaíma*, generally held to be the other principal work of early experimentalist Brazilian fiction, has accurately been described as a book without successors. See Haroldo de Campos, "Miramar na Mira," in *Memórias Sentimentais de João Miramar*, by Oswald de Andrade (São Paulo: Difusão Européia do Livro, 1964), pp. 10–11; Wilson Martins, *O Modernismo*, A Literatura Brasileira, vol. VI (São Paulo: Cultrix, 1965), p. 185. Not all critics in Brazil were willing to concede such importance to Guimarães Rosa, even after the publication of *Corpo de Baile*, however. At the time, one who felt that he was both a one-book author (because *Corpo de Baile* seemed to him to be a series of glued-together short stories) and a great "minor writer" was Wilson Martins. See his "50 Anos de Literatura Brasileira," *Panorama das Literaturas das Américas* (Nova Lisboa [Angola]: Município de Nova Lisboa, 1958), I, 190–95.

2. João Guimarães Rosa, *Corpo de Baile*, 2 vols. (Rio de Janeiro: José Olympio, 1956). All citations from *Corpo de Baile* are from the second edition (1960). There is also a third edition, in three volumes, all by José Olympio: *Manuelzão e Miguilim* (1964), *No Urubùquaquá, No Pinhém* (1965), and *Noites do Sertão* (1965). The translations are mine. In the case of

titles and short phrases, I have attempted to approximate the *sense* of the original rather than the poetry.

3. Oswaldino Marques, *A Seta e o Alvo* (Rio de Janeiro: Ministério da Educação e Cultura, 1957), p. 21.

4. One of the best is Franklin de Oliveira, "Guimarães Rosa," in *A Literatura no Brasil*, vol. V, direção de Afrânio Coutinho (Rio de Janeiro: Sul Americana, 1970), pp. 402–49. Like most of the general studies on Guimarães Rosa, the bulk of the study is devoted to *Grande Sertão*. Another fairly extensive study is Willi Bolle's chapter on *Corpo de Baile*, entitled "Anguished Consciences," which deals principally with the internalization of rural living conditions. Bolle, *Fórmula*, pp. 65–82.

5. Cassiano Ricardo, "Discurso na Sessão de Saudade," *Em Memória de João Guimarães Rosa* (Rio de Janeiro: José Olympio, 1968), p. 123.

6. Among them are the invention of collective nouns, the frequent employ of certain suffixes for the formation of neologisms (*-al, ã, -im*), the use of the portmanteau word, the invention of new nominal forms from verb roots, reduplication, inversion of word order, onomatopoeia, and alliteration. Daniel, *Travessia*, pp. 44, 46, 48, 50, 59, 64, 89, 104, 139, 141.

7. "Baroque" here is used in its broadest sense, and in part because of the frequency with which it appears as a description of Guimarães Rosa's works. Obviously the term "mannerist" could be applied as well, since "baroque" has both chronological and stylistic connotations, and may imply more than its user intended. The decorative effect in *Corpo de Baile* is nevertheless accompanied by an internal cohesion more characteristically "baroque" than "mannerist."

8. These examples are all from the first two pages of "Cara-de-Bronze," cited above. The last element mentioned, meter, is an especially interesting subject. Mary Daniel points out that, strictly speaking, meter (or more exactly, metric feet), has never been important in poetry written in Portuguese. Guimarães Rosa employs metric feet with some frequency, especially in this book and in *Sagarana*. His favorite seems to be the trochee. Professor Daniel cites another example (in trochaic dimeter) in "Estória de Amor," but all the tales in the book contain examples of this technique. Daniel, p. 153.

9. It has been shown that language is, in fact, the principal terminus of effect in some of the "new novels" of Spanish America. In these novels, language can be construed as an anarchic creative force made intelligible by structure. Raymond D. Souza, "Language vs. Structure in the Contemporary Spanish American Novel," *Hispania* 52, no. 4 (December, 1969), 833–39. *Corpo de Baile* can be read in this fashion, but I think that Guimarães Rosa's use of language is not so intentionally histrionic, because rather than attempting to suggest something like "the chaos of modern existence," his preoccupation is with an implied order of things. Linguistic

and structural invention are made necessary by the unaccustomed nature of that order. Rather than a mannerism or a merely stylistic affectation, as is the case with some of the Spanish Americans, random order in Guimarães Rosa's work is the result of a complex but nevertheless coherent view of reality.

10. One indication of the complexity of this tale has been examined by a Brazilian critic, who notes that the opening sequences of the story have Pedro and his entourage stopping at a different ranch each day for a week. Each ranch has a symbolic name, at each Pedro interacts with a companion with a related name, and there is for each place a god, an attribute, a planet, and an event connected with the locale. On Tuesday, for example, which is the day of Mars, the god of war, they stay at the ranch of Marciano, Pedro goes out with his friend Martinho, and there is a fight. All the other days have equally related sequences of symbol and attribute. Ana Maria Machado, *O Recado do Nome* (Rio de Janeiro: Imago, 1976), pp. 106–15.

11. See Benedito Nunes, "O Amor na Obra de Guimarães Rosa," *Revista do Livro*, no. 26 (September, 1964), pp. 43–44.

12. Guimarães Rosa's preoccupation with symbolic detail led him to participate in every phase of the publication of his books. He once reportedly spent seven hours on the phone discussing with the artist (Poty) the cover design for *Corpo de Baile*. His passion for the *buriti* as a symbol is apparent in several editions of his various works. He asked the publishers to eliminate the biographical notes about himself for the first edition of this book and to replace them with an essay on the *buriti* written by Afonso Arinos, and in a planned publication containing speeches and documents pertaining to his work, he asked the publisher personally to include among the illustrations a "nice big" *buriti*. "Nota da Editora," *Em Memória*, pp. 8–10. An extremely convoluted but perceptive analysis of the symbolic uses of the *buriti* in this particular proem can be found in Luís Costa Lima, "O Buriti entre os Homens ou o Exílio da Utopia," *A Metamorfose do Silêncio* (Rio de Janeiro: Eldorado, 1974), pp. 129–79.

13. Franklin de Oliveira has referred to the tales in *Corpo de Baile* as "adult fairy tales," in part because of the importance of myth and symbol. As Maurice Capovilla observes, the adult segment is provided in part by the seriousness of the game. "O Recado do Morro," a kind of mystery story, is comparable to a children's game, in which whoever makes a mistake is a dunce. Here, if the character fails to solve the mystery on time, he dies. Oliveira, "Guimarães Rosa," p. 425; Maurice Capovilla, " 'O Recado do Morro', de João Guimarães Rosa," *Revista do Livro*, no. 25 (March, 1964), pp. 132, 140.

14. Rui Mourão suggests that the footnotes transform the tale into a kind of scientific treatise, "a speculative thesis." Rui Mourão, "Processo da Linguagem, Processo do Homem, em 'Cara-de-Bronze'," *Luso-Brazilian Review* 4, no. 1 (Spring, 1967), 77. Heitor Martins has shed some light on the

structure and mysterious title of this tale. He suggests that the title is similar to the titles of Byzantine romances in that it refers to the locality where the action takes place, and that there are a number of structural hints pointing toward an adaptation of the Oedipus myth. Martins, "No Urubùquaquá, em Colônia," *Revista Hispánica Moderna* 35, no. 3 (Jan.–April, 1969), 255–60. The most complete study of the tale is Benedito Nunes' "A Viagem do Grivo," *O Dorso do Tigre* (São Paulo: Perspectiva, 1969), pp. 181–95. This study is especially useful for its analysis of mythical and literary parallels.

15. Also in this tale, one of the minor characters answers a question about his "searching for words" with the apparently nonsensical "Aí, Zé, Ôpa!" meaning, roughly, "There, Joe, Wow!" But read backward, this line renders the Portuguese word for—"poetry." Rónai, cited by Nei Leandro de Castro, *Universo e Vocabulário do Grande Sertão* (Rio de Janeiro: José Olympio, 1970), p. 10, n. 16; Sperber, *Caos*, p. 61. Critics have discovered numerous other hidden clues in this tale. I have cited these examples only to provide an idea of the complexity and density of this particular proem.

16. Guimarães Rosa reportedly once told Pedro Xisto that the names he had given to characters while writing a tale at times substantially altered their character and thus their role in the action, which in turn often changed the outcome of a plot. As an example he cited Doralda. Pedro Xisto, "À Busca da Poesia," *Revista do Livro*, nos. 21–22 (March–June, 1961), p. 13, n. 23. Presumably if her nuclear name had been Dola or Dadá and Doralda merely one of the satellite names, "Dão-Lalalão" would have been a different story. This particular character is, in fact, the focus of a chapter on the "sensorial name" in Machado's *Recado do Nome*, pp. 173–81. One interesting conclusion in this naming analysis is that phonetic components of names seem to be intentionally grouped by Guimarães Rosa. She notes a predominance of liquids and nasals in names of characters marked by sensuality. Machado, p. 149.

17. These affective catalogs also occur in the text of the tales of *Corpo de Baile*, as in the alphabetized listing of names of those in attendance at the party in "Estória de Amor," p. 144. Guimarães Rosa's preoccupation with things and their names affects every aspect of his writing. Mary Daniel observes that by grammatical category, his prose is highly nominal, that his inventions and deformations are almost always in the direction of the noun. His interest in names and people and animals is thus more in their *being* than in their *doing*. Daniel, p. 84.

18. See Capovilla, pp. 133, 141–42.

19. This exploitation of insinuative potential is not, of course, new to fiction. Writers have long explored the suggestive possibilities of names, by giving the first clue to the physical appearance and personality of characters through careful naming. Frodo Baggins and Trout Fishing in America Shorty take on their first clear definition merely because of their names, and

certain traits and actions are also made impossible by their possession of such appellations. Guimarães Rosa's care in the choice of designations and alternative names is, however, developed to the point of suggesting that in many senses the name *is* the person. In *Corpo de Baile*, in fact, the dramatic importance of a character is often better revealed by his name than by what he does.

20. Note the scene of pp. 331–32, in which the dialogue, marking chronological time, is in italics, and the psychological process and time remain in roman type.

### Chapter Three

1. João Guimarães Rosa, *Grande Sertão: Veredas*, 4th ed. (Rio de Janeiro: José Olympio, 1965). References and citations from the original are from this edition. Because the title is long and somewhat clumsy, I have reduced it to initials and refer to it in this chapter as *GSV*. Because such reductions can be confusing in another context, I have in other chapters referred to the work as *Grande Sertão;* João Guimarães Rosa, *The Devil to Pay in the Backlands*, trans. by James L. Taylor and Harriet de Onís (New York: Knopf, 1963). The original title is probably unrenderable in English. The word *sertão*, itself untranslatable, is usually carried into English as "backlands" or "hinterland." It generally refers to an area in the interior of Northeast Brazil, particularly the extremely arid sections, but here it refers also to the northern part of the state of Minas Gerais. *Veredas* ordinarily means "paths," but it has a more restricted connotation referring to the wetlands in the *sertão* and another as "small river." Since all these meanings are probably intentional, given the importance of the quest in the book, a literal rendition would produce something like "Great Backlands: Watercourses/Paths," an exceedingly clumsy and unattractive title. The unfortunate connotation of the English title as that of an adventure story may be unavoidable, but it is nonetheless unfortunate. One of the book's most enthusiastic devotees has taken particular exception to the unwieldy title. Adolfo Casais Monteiro, "Guimarães Rosa: Uma Revolução no Romance Brasileiro," *O Romance* (Rio de Janeiro: José Olympio, 1964), p. 240.

2. Most Brazilian writers have favored parallels based on very general qualities, but some base their correspondences on point of view, character, language, narrative form, or epic-mythic overtones. The compulsion to compare the work to the masterpieces of world literature is so universal and wide-ranging that an incomplete but illustrative survey may be of use. Besides comparisons to almost every Brazilian novel ever written, usually to the advantage of *GSV*, Brazilian critics have attempted to situate the novel by comparison to the following appalling array of works: *Don Quixote*, Mann's *Dr. Faustus*, *Robinson Crusoe*, Joyce's *Ulysses*, Conrad's *Lord Jim*, Dostoevski's *The Idiot*, *The Decameron*, the *Canterbury Tales*, *The Arabian Nights*, the *Aeneid*, *Hamlet*, *Moby Dick*, the *Odyssey* and *The Holy Bible*.

These parallels and more can be found in Henriqueta Lisboa, "A Poesia de *Grande Sertão: Veredas,*" *Revista do Livro,* no. 12 (dezembro, 1958), pp. 142–44; José Hildebrando Dacanal, *Nova Narrativa Épica no Brasil* (Porto Alegre: Sulina, 1973), p. 11; Joel Pontes, "O Geralista Riobaldo," *O Aprendiz da Crítica* (Rio de Janeiro: INL, 1960), pp. 123, 135; Monteiro, "Guimarẽs Rosa," pp. 236, 240; Dante Moreira Leite, "Grande Sertão: Veredas," *O Amor Romântico e Outros Temas* (São Paulo: Conselho Estadual de Cultura, 1964), p. 61; Irlemar Chiampi Cortez, "Narração e Metalinguagem em *Grande Sertão Veredas,*" *Língua e Literatura,* no. 2 (1973), p. 65, n. 9; José Hildebrando Dacanal, *Realismo Mágico* (Porto Alegre: Ed. Movimento, 1970), p. 22; Castro, *Universo,* p. 6.

3. Monteiro, "Guimarães Rosa," pp. 236, 238.

4. Eduardo Portella, "Um Romance e Sua Dialética," *Dimensões I,* 2nd ed. (Rio de Janeiro: Agir, 1959), p. 79.

5. Meir Sternberg, "What is Exposition?" in *The Theory of the Novel: New Essays,* ed. John Halperin (New York: Oxford Unversity Press, 1974), pp. 35–36. Sternberg faults the Russian Formalists for failing to consider the importance of the manipulation of point of view as a multiplying factor of the *sujet.* He also discusses at some length the fallacy of reducing the concept of *fabula* to "story" and that of *sujet* simply to "plot," pp. 37–41.

6. See Roberto Schwarz, "Grande Sertão: A Fala," *A Sereia e o Desconfiado* (Rio de Janeiro: Civilização Brasileira, 1965), p. 24; Wilson Martins, "Guimarães Rosa na Sala de Aula," in Daniel, *Travessia,* p. xxiii.

7. Walnice Nogueira Galvão, *As Formas do Falso* (São Paulo: Perspectiva, 1972), pp. 69–70. It would not, however, be altogether unproductive to conduct an experiment in which the text of the book would be read to illiterate Brazilians and their reactions analyzed. It is not easy to predict what conclusions might be extracted from such an experiment, but the plausibility of the project is itself a minor commentary on the character of the book's diction.

8. Sternberg, "What is Exposition?" p. 42.

9. Cortez, "Narração e Metalinguagem," pp. 69–71.

10. Antônio Cândido, "Ser Jagunço em Guimarães Rosa," *Revista Iberoamericana de literatura,* 2nd series, vol. 2, no. 2 (1970), p. 69.

11. E[mir] R[odríguez] Monegal, "The Contemporary Brazilian Novel," *Fiction in Several Languages,* ed. Henri Peyre (Boston: Houghton Mifflin, 1968), p. 9.

12. Cândido, "Ser Jagunço," p. 65.

13. A curious study which examines this relationship in rather too much depth uses a series of pseudomathematical equations to suggest that the design is in fact so complex that the reader is actually the author of the novel, a provocative but not very functional proposition along the lines of the old song "I'm My Own Grandpa." See Cortez, "Narração e Metalinguagem," esp. pp. 90–91.

14. Daniel, *Travessia*, pp. 105, 68.

15. See M. Cavalcanti Proença's pioneering study "Trilhas no Grande Sertão," in *Augusto dos Anjos e Outros Ensaios* (Rio de Janeiro: José Olympio, 1959), pp. 151–241. A listing and analysis of these and other categories can be found on pp. 213–34.

16. Martins, "50 Anos," pp. 198–202.

17. I personally believe such claims of stylistic inaccessibility to be overstated, but Henriqueta Lisboa calls the book an "arduous" task and claims that foreigners would find it extremely difficult to understand. Lisboa, "A Poesia de *GSV*," p. 141. Autran Dourado, himself a novelist, notes that a lot of critics were taken in by Guimarães Rosa's "con game" *(conto do vigário)* and led to believe that genuine regionalisms were invented words and erudite inventions were regionalisms. Autran Dourado, "Guimarães Rosa: Barroco e Coloquial," *Uma Poética de Romance* (São Paulo: Perspectiva, 1973), pp. 52–53. Ivana Versiani sees Guimarães Rosa's grammar not as simply a random deformation, but as a "co-system," in which ungrammatical forms can be used to indicate, among other things, the psychic attitude of the speaker. Versiani, "Para a Sintaxe de *Grande Sertão: Veredas*," in Coelho and Versiani, *Dois Estudos*, p. 110. One of the most interesting anecdotes on the matter of linguistic comprehension is recounted by Adolfo Casais Monteiro. He relates that Guimarães Rosa one day found himself in a conversation with one of his nonreaders, who claimed that the book was unintelligible. Guimarães Rosa, noting that the man was carrying a book in French, asked permission to look at the book. Noting that his critical friend was a hundred-odd pages into the work, Guimarães Rosa started asking him the meaning of various words he had just read. Finding him unable to define a number of them, Guimarães Rosa extracted the logical conclusion that if the man could understand French without knowing all the words, he should be able to understand (Guimarães Rosa's) Portuguese, his native language. Monteiro, "Guimarães Rosa," p. 239.

18. Javier Domingo, "João Guimarães Rosa y la alegría," *Revista do Livro*, No. 17 (March, 1960), p. 61.

19. *Pequeno Dicionário Brasileiro da Língua Portuguesa*, 11th ed. (Rio de Janeiro: Civilização Brasileira, 1967).

20. The *Pequeno Dicionário* lists nineteen synonyms and ninety-eight euphemisms for the devil, p. 108. Roget lists a total of nineteen in both categories, some rather obscure. Norman Lewis, ed., *The New Roget's Thesaurus in Dictionary Form* (New York: G. P. Putnam's Sons, 1961) p. 110.

21. Xisto lists at least sixty-nine names in *GSV* which clearly refer to the devil, another handful which by their context and form probably do likewise. Xisto, "À Busca da Poesia," pp. 23–24.

22. José Carlos Garbuglio, *O Mundo Movente de Guimarães Rosa* (São Paulo: Ática, 1972), p. 56.

23. Tristão de Athayde, "Satã nas Letras," *Meio Século*, pp. 100, 109.

Athayde claims that Otávio de Faria and Guimarães Rosa were the first two Brazilian writers in whose work the devil appears as a character, or at least as the central reality of the work (p. 91).

24. See M. Cavalcanti Proença's "Dom Riobaldo do Urucúia, Cavaleiro dos Campos Gerais," in "Trilhas," pp. 161–76, esp. pp. 164–70; Antônio Cândido, "O Homem dos Avessos," *Tese e Antítese* (São Paulo: Ed. Nacional, 1964), pp. 119–40, esp. 131–33; José Carlos Garbuglio, *Literatura e Realidade Brasileira* (São Paulo: Conselho Estadual de Cultura, 1970), pp. 16–28.

25. Walnice Nogueira Galvão notes that the conceit of comparing the leather-clad Brazilian cowboy to the medieval knight (because of the bronze color of the dress and presumed heroic character of the men) derives from Euclides da Cunha's *Os Sertões. Formas do Falso*, p. 53. The moralizing qualities of the narrative are commented on by Luís Costa Lima, "O Sertão e o Mundo: Têrmos da Vida," *Por que Literatura* (Petrópolis: Vozes, 1966), pp. 79–80. José Hildebrando Dacanal takes exception to all these generalities in a somewhat overliteral historical reading, in which he objects to comparisons of the medieval world to a country full of hillbillies and the Middle Ages to the "post-European age." Especially attuned to anachronism, he views the parallel to the Grail legend untenable in part because the interlocutor drives around in a jeep. Dacanal, *Nova Narrativa*, p. 29.

26. The argumentation over this point has been long and at times tedious. The serious scholar may discover that such-and-such motif is a rewrite of some Finnish folktale or that there exists a medieval romance in which the motif sequence is identical to a passage of the novel. This kind of information may be useful to the reader, and may even enhance a subsequent rereading. But to discover and prove that *The Lord of the Rings* is an allegory on World War II or that *Gravity's Rainbow* is a work without precedent is merely curious or picturesque—it is neither useful nor particularly enlightening. The difference, unfortunately, appears simply to be one of good sense: to prove that assorted features may derive from earlier traditions than expected may increase the reader's awareness and interest, but to deny flatly such possibilities on the basis of trivialities, or to assert plagiarism, is not only a disservice to the reader but a deadend for the critic.

27. Ernst Robert Curtius notes that the convention of the epic as a nautical voyage was common in the Roman epic, and the comparison of the poet to a sailor and sailing the seas as a dangerous business was observed even by Dante. *European Literature and the Latin Middle Ages*, trans. Willard R. Trask (Princeton University Press, 1967), pp. 128–30. M. Cavalcanti Proença comments on the symbolic significance of the sea in *GSV* but does not link this phenomenon to epic tradition. "Trilhas," pp. 186–87, 207–10.

28. See Curtius, *European Literature*, p. 172, for an enumeration of the traditional characteristics of epic heroes.

29. Cândido, "Ser Jagunço," p. 67.

30. See Curtius' essay on "Etymology as a Category of Thought," in *European Literature*, pp. 495–500, in which mention is made of the habit of giving characters names which may not reveal much except by sometimes rather obscure etymology.

31. Cavalcanti Proença, "Trilhas," pp. 178–79, 186–87.

32. Gilberto Freyre, *New World in the Tropics: The Culture of Modern Brazil* (New York: Random House, 1963), p. 218. Another study notes the meaning of *baldo* as possibly indicating "audacity, daring," but the etymology is not mentioned. Júlia Conceição Fonseca Santos, *Nomes de Personagens em Guimarães Rosa* (Rio de Janeiro: INL, 1971), pp. 151–57.

33. Santos, *Nomes*, pp. 113–20.

34. Garbuglio, *Mundo*, p. 73. One writer has even unearthed a Japanese origin for the name Diadorim, which he claims means "(ancient) imperial palace." William Myron Davis, "Japanese Elements in *Grande Sertão: Veredas*," *Romance Philology* 29, no. 4 (May, 1976), 418.

35. Cândido, "Ser Jagunço," p. 61.

36. Garbuglio, *Mundo*, p. 55, 115.

37. See Oskar Seyffert, *A Dictionary of Classical Antiquities* (1891; Cleveland: World Publishing Co., 1956), pp. 286–88.

38. Enigma and totality are clearly suggested in various ways in the book, the most obvious being the use of the infinity symbol on the last page, a sign also used in *Sagarana*. The most complete study of the amorous and erotic phenomena in *GSV* is Nunes, "O Amor," pp. 39–62. Nunes suggests that Diadorim reflects the ancients' idea of androgyny as a plenitude, a completeness most ordinary beings have lost. (56). A somewhat more eccentric view is that of Paulo Hecker Filho, who faults Guimarães Rosa for his failure to carry through the "real theme" of the work, which he identifies as homosexual love. Hecker Filho, "Grande Romance: Frustrações," *Suplemento Literário do Estado de São Paulo*, no. 822 (April 29, 1973), p. 5.

39. Daniel, *Travessia*, p. 10.

40. Garbuglio, *Mundo*, pp. 80, 124.

41. Leite, "GSV," *Amor Romântico*, pp. 66–72.

42. Fábio Lucas, *O Caráter Social da Literatura Brasileira* (Rio de Janeiro: Paz e Terra, 1970), pp. 93–95.

43. Antônio Cândido's first review of *GSV* compared the composition of the book to the process Béla Bartók used in forging an erudite, extremely refined music based on folk music. "Homem dos Avessos," p. 122. The recognitional responses of this source-fusion are produced in all of Guimarães Rosa's work, perhaps most notably in *Sagarana*. The musical comparison is a relevant one, and might by extension be applied to composers closer to home, such as Aaron Copland in the U.S. or Heitor Villa-Lobos in Brazil.

44. Authored by Manoel D'Almeida Filho (São Paulo: Prelúdio, n.d.).

45. Oliveira, "Guimarães Rosa," p. 436. Several writers have advanced

the theory that *GSV* was, in fact, originally intended as another of the "tales" in *Corpo de Baile*.

## Chapter Four

1. João Guimarães Rosa, *Primeiras Estórias*, 3rd ed. (Rio de Janeiro: José Olympio, 1967). In this chapter, hereafter referred to as *PE*; João Guimarães Rosa, *The Third Bank of the River and Other Stories*, trans. Barbara Shelby (New York: Knopf, 1968). Quotations are from this translation.

2. Luis Harss and Barbara Dohmann, *Into the Mainstream: Conversations With Latin-American Writers* (New York: Harper & Row, 1967), p. 170.

3. Bolle, *Fórmula*, pp. 83–109.

4. The concept of the liminal phase and the liminal persona is a complex one, but the emphasis on threshold states and threshold characters is so great in this book that the anthropological construct seems a useful generality. Victor Turner enumerates some of the characteristics of liminality which seem most suited to this application. In addition to his observation that liminality is an ontological state, in which the reflective threshold-being is expected to develop new perceptions of the relationships in his world, Turner notes the following features: liminality as an interstructural situation in which the liminal persona passes through a realm which has none of the attributes of the previous or coming state; the transformative aspects of liminality; the use of special names and symbols in conjunction with liminality; the emphasis on the transition itself rather than on the previous or coming state; the ambiguous and paradoxical nature of liminality; the frequency of vehicles which combine animal and human characteristics; the isolation and freedom from ordinary social constraints applied to persons in the liminal state. Victor Turner, "Betwixt and Between: The Liminal Period in *Rites de Passage*," *The Forest of Symbols* (Ithaca, New York: Cornell University Press, 1967), pp. 93–99, 105. Reference will be made to a number of these features in this chapter.

5. *Saudade*, a word Portuguese speakers point to as the least translatable in their lexicon, involves a relishing of the passage of time, a voluptuous melancholy for people absent and places distant.

6. Bolle, *Fórmula*, p. 93.

7. José Geraldo Nougueira Moutinho, "Primeiras Estórias," in *A Procura do Número* (São Paulo: Conselho Estadual de Cultura, 1967), p. 77.

8. Lucas, *O Caráter Social*, pp. 26–27.

9. Daniel, *Travessia*, pp. 59, 66, 108, 114.

10. Willi Bolle's analysis, conducted after the manner of the Russian formalists and French structuralists, is a good example. Bolle notes that there are several features of these narratives which complicate structural analysis: the apparent eccentricity of the characters, the fantastic dimension

(coded as *imag*, and used in his formulas to represent imagined, fantastic, or inventive features of a tale), and the fact that "stylistic elements [become] units of the fabula," Bolle, *Fórmula*, pp. 83–109, esp. p. 86.

11. Nunes, "O Amor," p. 47, note 26.

## Chapter Five

1. João Guimarães Rosa, *Tutaméia (Terceiras Estórias)*, (Rio de Janeiro: José Olympio, 1967). All citations are to this edition. Translations are mine.

2. Bolle, *Fórmula*, p. 112.

3. Ana Maria Machado noted the author's initials in this sequence, and, pursuing the clue further, discovered that the initial letters of the prefaces can be rearranged to spell "Hans," the German equivalent of João. In addition, she claims, the point at which the alphabetical order is broken is merely part of a "warning" issued by the author. Reading the full titles of the two preceding stories, then the initials, then the full title of the subsequent tale produces: "Hiato: intruge-se JGR lá nas campinas," (Hiatus: J[oão] G[uimarães] R[osa] is deceiving [or telling lies] out there in the country.") Machado, *Recado*, p. 92, note 3.

4. Bolle, *Fórmula*, pp. 111–33.

5. Ibid., pp. 116–17, 120–21, 124–27, 130–31. Another plausible grouping of the tales might be found in Guimarães Rosa's indexing scheme. That is, there might be four groups of tales each related to the preceding preface, which could produce categories such as tales related to nothingness, word transformation tales, skewed perception tales, and illusion/reality tales. Because of the intricacies of the prefaces and the interdependency of the conceits in them, however, the application of this scheme requires considerable dexterity. One interesting attempt along these lines is Judith Grossman, "João Guimarães Rosa, *Tutaméia*, Fecha-te Sésamo da Obra," *Cadernos Brasileiros*, no. 56 (Nov.–Dec., 1969), pp. 5–23.

6. Daniel, *Travessia*, p. 182.

7. Assis Brasil, *Guimarães Rosa* (Rio de Janeiro: Simões, 1969), pp. 74–75.

8. Ibid., pp. 74–75; Paulo Hecker Filho, "Situação do Conto Atual," *Suplemento Literário do Estado de São Paulo*, no. 811 (February 11, 1973), p. 1.

9. Eneida Maria de Souza notes that the relationship of humor to reality is comparable to the relationship between art and reality, the difference lying principally in the relative breadth of the frontiers. In her analysis, Guimarães Rosa's constant sense of irony is a humorous attitude toward, among other things, language itself. She goes on to discuss *Tutaméia* as representative of what she calls a "carnivalization of the concept of art," since it presents life "backward," abolishing distinctions between the sacred and the profane, the sublime and the insignificant. Souza, "Ficção,

Realidade e Humor em *Tutaméia*," *Suplemento Literário de Minas Gerais* (August 10, 1974), pp. 8–9.

10. Eneida Souza notes the concept of contradictions in coexistence as a feature of the third preface. Ibid., p. 9.

11. Lima connects the aphorism to what he calls the *relato mítico*, a kind of folk locution which encloses elements of community wisdom or has a myth's effect of justifying the prevailing order of things. Lima, "Mito e Provérbio em Guimarães Rosa," *Metamorfose*, pp. 51–52, 57.

### Chapter Six

1. João Guimarães Rosa, *Estas Estórias* (Rio de Janeiro: José Olympio, 1969). All citations are from this edition. Translations are mine.

2. *Seleta de João Guimarães Rosa*, Organização, estudo e notas por Paulo Rónai (Rio de Janeiro: José Olympio, 1973), p. 108.

3. See Rónai, "Nota Introdutória," in Guimarães Rosa, *Estas Estórias*, pp. xiii–xv for information on the publishing history of these stories.

4. Rónai, in *Seleta*, p. 108.

5. Hélio Pólvora, *A Fôrça da Ficção* (Petrópolis: Vozes, 1971), pp. 26–27.

6. See Haroldo de Campos, "A Linguagem do Iauaretê," in *Guimarães Rosa em Três Dimensões* (São Paulo: Conselho Estadual de Cultura, 1970), for a discussion of linguistic aspects of this story. Campos discusses this metamorphosis but does not mention that other writers have achieved similar changes through linguistic manipulation. One writer who has employed a similar process is the Guatemalan Miguel Ángel Asturias.

7. Oswaldino Marques writes that rather than a descriptivist treatment, this tale provides an example of Guimarães Rosa's talent for dislocating point of view in stories about animals from the human perspective to the perspective of the animals themselves, making reality appear to be a "faunosphere." "Guimarães Rosa—Cineasta," in *Ensaios Escolhidos* (Rio de Janeiro: Civilização Brasileira, 1968), p. 149. Hélio Pólvora asserts that Brazilians all tend toward either zoophilia or zoophobia, which would intensify reader reaction to the "zooerasty" in this tale. Pólvora, *Fôrça*, p. 25. Undoubtedly most cultures establish particular boundaries for man-animal relationships, but Pólvora's observation is probably correct, especially in a story in which the animal is one which the national mythology has invested with such importance.

8. Paulo Rónai, in the preface to *Estas Estórias*, p. xiv, claims that it was first published in 1947, five years before Guimarães Rosa made the trip which supposedly provided the material. Most other writers mention 1952 as the first date of publication. If indeed it was published in 1947, its fictional aspects would be even more striking.

9. Roberto Simões refers to "With Cowboy Mariano" as a narrative still

in a "placental state." "Notícia da Visitação Realizada nas Veredas do *Grande Sertão," Diálogo*, no. 8 (November, 1957), p. 64.

### Chapter Seven

1. João Guimarães Rosa, *Ave, Palavra* (Rio de Janeiro: José Olympio, 1970). All citations are from this edition. The translations are mine.

2. The English rendition obviously misses some of the effects of the original, which contains a stressed syllable *av* in both words, a suggestive phonetic linkage system which in Portuguese is referred to as *palavra-puxa-palavra*, or "word-pulls-word." The technique is one frequently used by Guimarães Rosa. Since the system implies something beyond free association, all meaningful components of the words involved merit examination. *Ave* also means "bird" in Portuguese, and it is not unreasonable to assume that the characteristics of flight and elusiveness associated with birds may also have been intended in reference to "word." A faithful translation of the title would thus require that a sequence with the sonorous effect of "bird, word" plus the laudatory conceptualization included in "hail" be proposed.

3. Paulo Rónai, "Nota Introdutória," *Ave, Palavra*, no page.

4. Assis Brasil, *A Nova Literatura* [vol. I—O Romance] (Rio de Janeiro: Americana, 1973), p. 66.

# Selected Bibliography

The bibliography on Guimarães Rosa is so extensive that a complete listing is virtually impossible. The special volume issued by Livraria José Olympio to honor the writer *(Em Memória de João Guimarães Rosa)*, for example, contains a bibliography compiled by Plínio Doyle which runs to almost nine hundred items. In the following list I have included principally book-length studies along with articles of particular importance or unusual perspective. I have not attempted to list the literally hundreds of articles which appear in Brazilian journals and newspapers, because they are of very limited accessibility in this country, and a number of the better pieces have by now appeared as chapters in books. The two most important sources in newspaper format are the *Suplemento Literário* of the *Estado de São Paulo* (now defunct), and the *Suplemento Literário* of Minas Gerais, both of which have issued special numbers dedicated to Guimarães Rosa.

Where substantially the same material appears in more than one place, I have cited the one likely to be most accessible and noted the others, and I have indicated, where appropriate, that items contain further bibliographical information.

## PRIMARY SOURCES

1. Works in order of publication (editions are those used in this study).
*Sagarana.* 7th ed. Rio de Janeiro: José Olympio, 1965.
*Corpo de Baile.* 2nd ed. Rio de Janeiro: José Olympio, 1960. Subsequent editions appear in three volumes: *Manuelzão e Miguilim, No Urubùquaquá, No Pinhém,* and *Noites do Sertão.*
*Grande Sertão: Veredas.* 4th ed. Rio de Janeiro: José Olympio, 1965.
*Primeiras Estórias.* 3rd ed. Rio de Janeiro: José Olympio, 1967.
*Tutaméia (Terceiras Estórias).* Rio de Janeiro: José Olympio, 1967.
*Estas Estórias.* Rio de Janeiro: José Olympio, 1969.
*Ave, Palavra.* Rio de Janeiro: José Olympio, 1970.

2. Translations
*Sagarana.* Translated by Harriet de Onís, introduction by Franklin de Oliveira. New York: Alfred A. Knopf, 1966.

173

*The Devil to Pay in the Backlands (Grande Sertão: Veredas)*. Translated by James L. Taylor and Harriet de Onís. New York: Alfred A. Knopf, 1963.

*The Third Bank of the River and Other Stories (Primeiras Estórias)*. Translated by Barbara Shelby. New York: Alfred A. Knopf, 1968.

SECONDARY SOURCES

BOLLE, WILLI. *Fórmula e Fábula: Teste de uma Gramática Narrativa, Aplicada aos Contos de Guimarães Rosa*. São Paulo: Editora Perspectiva, [1973]. Structuralist analysis of the short stories through *Tutaméia*, combined with a curious sociological slant in the interpretive sections.

*Books Abroad* 44, no. 1 (Winter, 1970), 7–50. This special number on "The Latin American Novel Today" is a good starting point for readers unfamiliar with the subject. Of particular interest are Emir Rodríguez-Monegal's article, "The New Latin American Novel," pp. 45–50, and Gregory Rabassa's "João Guimarães Rosa: The Third Bank of the River," pp. 30–36.

BRASIL, [FRANCISCO DE] ASSIS. *Guimarães Rosa*. Rio de Janeiro: Organização Simões Editora, 1969. Very general.

————. *A Nova Literatura: vol. I—O Romance*. Rio de Janeiro: Editora Americana, 1973. Guimarães Rosa, pp. 59–67. Also general, but useful for situating Guimarães Rosa in the context of modern Brazilian fiction.

CÂNDIDO, ANTÔNIO. "O Homem do Avessos." In *Tese e Antítese*. São Paulo: Editora Nacional, 1964, pp. 119–40. One of the clearest analyses of *Grande Sertão*, it departs from an examination of the sets of antithetical dualities in the novel. Also appears, somewhat abbreviated, in the periodical *Diálogo*, no. 8, pp. 5–18.

CAPOVILLA, MAURICE. " 'O Recado do Morro', de João Guimarães Rosa." *Revista do Livro*, no. 25 (March, 1964), pp. 131–42. Good analysis of one of the stories in *Corpo de Baile*.

CASTRO, NEI LEANDRO DE. *Universo e Vocabulário do Grande Sertão*. Rio de Janeiro: José Olympio, 1970. A glossary of the oddities of vocabulary in *Grande Sertão*, distinguishing between terms invented and those still in the active vocabulary in the Brazilian interior.

COELHO, NELLY NOVAES and IVANA VERSIANI. *Guimarães Rosa; Dois Estudos*. São Paulo: Edições Quíron/INL, 1975. Two interesting studies, largely on the originality of *Sagarana* and the style of *Grande Sertão*.

CORTEZ, IRLEMAR CHIAMPI. "Narração e Metalinguagem em *Grande Sertão: Veredas*." *Língua e Literatura*, no. 2, [São Paulo], 1973, pp. 63–91. Semiotic investigation of rhetorical design in *Grande Sertão*.

DACANAL, JOSÉ HILDEBRANDO. *Nova Narrativa Épica no Brasil*. Porto Alegre: Editora Sulina, 1973. Focuses on *Grande Sertão*. Marred by an excess of obscure jargon.

————. *Realismo Mágico* (Porto Alegre: Movimento, 1970). Contains a long study on *Grande Sertão*, concluding that it represents a contribution to the Third World's ascendancy in literature.

DANIEL, MARY L. *João Guimarães Rosa: Travessia Literária* (Rio de Janeiro: José Olympio, 1968). Basically linguistic, but still one of the best studies to date. Bibliography.

————. "João Guimarães Rosa." *Studies in Short Fiction* 8, no. 1 (Winter, 1971), 209–16. A handsomely written and perceptive introduction to Guimarães Rosa's prose. Though brief, it contains the most lucid assessment of his style to appear in any language.

————. "Word Formation and Deformation in *Grande Sertão: Veredas.*" *Luso-Brazilian Review* 2, no. 1 (Summer, 1965), 81–97. One of the few sources in English on the subject.

DANTAS, PAULO. *Sagarana Emotiva: Cartas de J. Guimarães Rosa.* São Paulo: Livraria Duas Cidades, 1975. Letters from Guimarães Rosa to Dantas. Interesting biographical sidelights.

*Diálogo* (Revista de Cultura), no. 8 (November, 1957). A special number on Guimarães Rosa, with ten pieces on various facets of the work. Mainly useful for a sense of the impact of Guimarães Rosa's books just after publication.

FOSTER, DAVID WILLIAM and VIRGINIA RAMOS FOSTER, eds. *Modern Latin American Literature*, 2 vols. New York: Frederick Ungar, 1975. Guimarães Rosa, II, 282–95. Though uncritically organized, these selections are among the very few interpretive fragments on Guimarães Rosa which have been translated to English.

FREIXEIRO, FÁBIO. *Da Razão à Emoção.* São Paulo: Companhia Editora Nacional, 1968. Contains two interesting and informative articles on *Sagarana* and *Corpo de Baile.*

GALVÃO, WALNICE NOGUEIRA. *As Formas do Falso.* São Paulo: Editora Perspectiva, 1972. Carries the subtitle "A study of ambiguity in *Grande Sertão: Veredas,*" and, as such, is quite good.

GARBUGLIO, JOSÉ CARLOS. *O Mundo Movente de Guimarães Rosa.* São Paulo: Editora Ática, 1972. Another analysis of dualities in *Grande Sertão.* Bibliography.

GRIECO, AGRIPPINO. *Poetas e Prosadores do Brasil.* Rio de Janeiro: Editora Conquista, 1968. Contains a short piece, pp. 276–78, which is an interesting example of negative reaction to *Sagarana.*

*Guimarães Rosa (Ciclo de Conferências).* Belo Horizonte: Centro de Estudos Mineiros, 1966. Text of four papers on various aspects of the work.

GUIMARÃES ROSA, JOÃO. *Seleta.* Organization, study, and notes by Professor Paulo Rónai. Rio de Janeiro: José Olympio, 1973. Anthology, but the introduction and chronology are useful and the notes give an idea of how difficult Guimarães Rosa is for native speakers. Bibliography.

HARSS, LUIS, and BARBARA DOHMANN. *Into the Mainstream (Conversations with Latin-American Writers)*. New York: Harper & Row, 1967. Guimarães Rosa, pp. 137–72, is the only Brazilian included. This interview-based study is only vaguely useful in a critical sense, but it is interesting reading, and the few factual errors do not detract from its value as an introduction to Guimarães Rosa.

HAMILTON, RUSSELL G., Jr. "The Contemporary Brazilian Short Story." In *To Find Something New: Studies in Contemporary Literature*, edited by Henry Grosshans. Pullman: Washington State University Press, 1969. Pp. 118–35. Contains an intelligent review of the genre's importance in Brazil and perceptive remarks on some of the tales in *Tutaméia* (pp. 131–35).

LEITE, DANTE MOREIRA. *O Amor Romântico e Outros Temas*. São Paulo: Conselho Estadual de Cultura, 1964. Contains a psychological reading of *Grande Sertão*, pp. 61–72.

LIMA, LUÍS COSTA. *A Metamorfose do Silêncio*. Rio de Janeiro: Eldorado, 1974. Contains two semiotic studies, one on myth and proverb, another on the story "Buriti" from *Corpo de Baile*.

LORENZ, GÜNTER W. "Diálogo con Guimarães Rosa." *Mundo Nuevo*, no. 45 (March, 1970), pp. 27–47. Fascinating and occasionally illuminating interview.

MACHADO, ANA MARIA. *Recado do Nome: Leitura de Guimarães Rosa à Luz do Nome de Seus Personagens*. Rio de Janeiro: Imago Editora, 1976. Semiotic study. One of the best on the symbolism of names.

MARQUES, OSWALDINO. "Canto e Plumagem das Palavras." In *A Seta e o Alvo*. Rio de Janeiro: Instituto Nacional do Livro, 1957. Pp. 9–128. One of the pioneer studies, the focus of this work is principally *Sagarana*, the analytical method linguistic. Though weakened by some impressionistic passages, it is still valuable. It also appears in Marques' *Ensaios Escolhidos* (Rio de Janeiro: Civilização Brasileira, 1968), pp. 77–147.

MARTINS, WILSON. "50 Anos de Literatura Brasileira." In *Panorama das Literaturas das Américas*. Nova Lisboa (Angola): Município de Nova Lisboa, 1958. Vol. I, pp. 103–41. An early view of regionalist aspects of the first three works, mostly negative.

———. "Structural Perspectivism in Guimarães Rosa." In *The Brazilian Novel*, edited by Heitor Martins. Bloomington: Indiana University Publications, 1976. Pp. 59–76. One of the most lucid presentations of Guimarães Rosa as a writer "born classic." Also available as a separatum published by the Ibero-American Language and Area Center of New York University (Occasional Papers no. 3, 1973).

*Em Memória de João Guimarães Rosa*. Rio de Janeiro: José Olympio, 1968. Special volume issued as a tribute to Guimarães Rosa after his death.

Contains speeches, reprints of numerous studies, and extensive bibliography.

MONTEIRO, ADOLFO CASAIS. *O Romance (Teoria e Crítica).* Rio de Janeiro: José Olympio, 1964. Pages 235–47 contain an excellent early assessment of Guimarães Rosa's impact on Brazilian letters.

NUNES, BENEDITO. *O Dorso do Tigre.* São Paulo: Editora Perspectiva, 1969. Contains five very useful studies on various works, the best of them on *Corpo de Baile.* One of these, "O Amor na Obra de Guimarães Rosa," appeared in the September, 1964, number of the *Revista do Livro* (no. 26, pp. 39–62).

OLIVEIRA, FRANKLIN DE. "Guimarães Rosa." In *A Literatura no Brasil,* edited by Afrânio Coutinho. Rio de Janeiro: Editorial Sul Americana, 1970. Vol. V, pp. 402–49. One of the best introductory statements on Guimarães Rosa. Bibliography. See also Oliveira's absorbing introduction to *Sagarana,* in the English edition of that book.

PEREZ, RENARD. *Escritores Brasileiros Contemporâneos.* Rio de Janeiro: Editora Civilização Brasileira, 1960. Useful for biographical material. Guimarães Rosa, pp. 179–84.

PROENÇA, M. CAVALCANTI. *Trilhas no Grande Sertão.* Rio de Janeiro: Instituto Nacional do Livro, 1958. Another of the pioneer analyses of *Grande Sertão,* this one contains considerable material on the medieval parallels and on language deformation. Also available in Proença's book *Augusto dos Anjos e Outros Ensaios* (Rio de Janeiro: José Olympio, 1959), pp. 151–241, and in abbreviated form in the *Revista do Livro,* no. 5 (March, 1957), pp. 37–54.

RIBEIRO, GILVAN P. "O Alegórico em Guimarães Rosa." In *Realismo e Anti-Realismo na Literatura Brasileira.* Rio de Janeiro: Editora Paz e Terra, 1974. Pp. 95–104. Lukacsian analysis, explaining how *Grande Sertão* is a failed work.

RÓNAI, PAULO. "Os Prefácios de *Tutaméia*" and "As Estórias de *Tutaméia.*" in *Tutaméia.* 3rd ed. Rio de Janeiro: José Olympio, 1969. Pp. 193–97 and 197–201, respectively. These two articles, which first appeared in the *Suplemento Literário* of the *Estado de São Paulo* (March 16 and March 23, 1968), are probably the most lucid treatments of this difficult book.

SANTOS, JÚLIA CONCEIÇÃO FONSECA. *Nomes de Personagens em Guimarães Rosa.* Rio de Janeiro: Instituto Nacional do Livro, 1971. Catalog of names, examining deviations from standard given names and surnames, etymologies, and parallel use of names of characters in different works.

SCHWARZ, ROBERTO. *A Sereia e o Desconfiado.* Rio de Janeiro: Civilização Brasileira, 1965. Contains two short but provocative pieces (pp. 23–27 and 28–36) on *Grande Sertão.*

SPERBER, SUZI FRANKL. *Caos e Cosmos: Leituras de Guimarães Rosa*. São
    Paulo: Duas Cidades, 1976. A curious study of philosophical influences
    on Guimarães Rosa's works, based on an analysis of the contents of his
    private library and the marginal notations found in those books. Bib-
    liography.
VIGGIANO, ALAN. *Itinerário de Riobaldo Tatarana*. Belo Horizonte: Editora
    Comunicacão/INL, 1974. Georgraphical tracing of the protagonist's
    travels in *Grande Sertão*. Maps.
XISTO, PEDRO, AUGUSTO DE CAMPOS, and HAROLDO DE CAMPOS. *Guimarães
    Rosa em Tres Dimensões*. São Paulo: Conselho Estadual de Cultura,
    1970. Three articles, all previously published: À Busca da Poesia," by
    Xisto, originally published in *Folha da Manhã* and later reprinted in
    the *Revista do Livro* (nos. 21–22, 1957); Augusto de Campos' "Um
    Lance de 'Dês' do Grande Sertão," an important study which appeared
    in the *Revista do Livro* in 1959 (no. 16); Haroldo de Campos' "A Lin-
    guagem do Iauaretê," which appeared in 1962 in the *Suplemento
    Literário* of the *Estado de São Paulo*.

# Index